GREATEST
MUSICAL PLACES
OF THE WORLD

IN ASSOCIATION WITH
TIMPSON

Also available

The 50 Greatest Bike Rides of the World

The 50 Greatest Dishes of the World

The 50 Greatest Wonders of the World

The 50 Greatest Road Trips

The 50 Greatest Westerns

The 50 Greatest Train Journeys of the World

The 50 Greatest Rugby Union Players of All Time

The 50 Greatest Beers of the World

The 50 Most Influential Britons of the Last 100 Years

The 50 Greatest Walks of the World

Geoff Hurst's Greats: England's 1966 Hero Selects His
Finest Ever Footballers

David Gower's Greatest Half-Century

GREATEST
MUSICAL PLACES
OF THE WORLD

SARAH WOODS

Published in the UK in 2017 by
Icon Books Ltd, Omnibus Business Centre,
39–41 North Road, London N7 9DP
email: info@iconbooks.com
www.iconbooks.com

Sold in the UK, Europe and Asia
by Faber & Faber Ltd, Bloomsbury House,
74–77 Great Russell Street,
London WC1B 3DA or their agents

Distributed in the UK, Europe and Asia
by Grantham Book Services, Trent Road,
Grantham NG31 7XQ

Distributed in Australia and New Zealand
by Allen & Unwin Pty Ltd,
PO Box 8500, 83 Alexander Street,
Crows Nest, NSW 2065

Distributed in South Africa by
Jonathan Ball, Office B4, The District,
41 Sir Lowry Road, Woodstock 7925

Distributed in India by Penguin Books India,
7th Floor, Infinity Tower – C, DLF Cyber City,
Gurgaon 122002, Haryana

Distributed in Canada by Publishers Group Canada,
76 Stafford Street, Unit 300, Toronto, Ontario M6J 2S1

Distributed in the USA by Publishers Group West,
1700 Fourth Street, Berkeley, CA 94710

ISBN: 978-178578-189-6

Images – see individual pictures

Typeset and designed by Simmons Pugh

Printed and bound in the UK by Clays Ltd, St Ives plc

ABOUT THE AUTHOR

Sarah Woods is the author of over a dozen travel books, a fellow of the Royal Geographical Society and a member of the British Guild of Travel Writers. She has won the prestigious BGTW 'Travel Guide Writer of the Year' award and has twice won the Kenneth Westcott Jones Award. As a travel presenter on British daytime TV, Sarah won the PSA prize for reportage in 2012. She is also the author of *The 50 Greatest Road Trips of the World* and *The 50 Greatest Bike Rides of the World* in this series.

CONTENTS

Africa

INTRODUCTION

As a soul-stirring force, music can soothe pain, mend hearts, rebel rouse, celebrate, woo and challenge, powering endorphins and adrenaline to unparalleled highs. It enhances travel, inspires change and transports us – spiritually and physically – to new places. We carry with us thousands of messages, anthems, choruses and refrains that, quite literally, have struck a chord.

Music is unifying, storytelling, culturally distinctive, decisive, homogenous, and life-changing. We, the fans, each have our own relationship with the music, the band or artist, the track or the album. Fandom is an exclusive club to which any one of us can join; all of us, anywhere in the world.

Certain places are musically significant for a variety of reasons: some for the songs that are sung there, others as the birthplace of a musical genius, many made famous by videos and album covers. Wherever you are in the world, there will be a musical Mecca nearby; from the high-energy, peppy pop bars of Korea; the juke-box joints of America; and the pieces of history left behind by the many legends who helped define music's pantheon: Vienna; to Berlin with its beatnik band haunts; New York with its fabled studios, venues and auditoriums, and Ghent's bluesy basement bars. London has its eclectic mix of singer-songwriters from all musical genres, Memphis its snake-hipped ghosts of rock 'n' roll history, and Iceland has its awe-inspiring landscape that has helped to create music that is second-to-none. Head out to the South American rolling plains where cowboy music is king, or to the honky-tonk, boot-scooting bars of Nashville. Check out Tennessee, with its musical mix of rock, country, bluegrass, jazz and more, or savour the places with secret musical relevance far off the main tourist drag with their iconic guitar riffs, choral giants, fine orchestral compositions and heavyweight gods of rock. From old-time gypsy folk and spontaneous jazzmen, to keyboard wizards with sonic boom, the foremost musical places to visit are seducing a growing number of music lovers prepared to journey further afield to follow in the footsteps of tunesmiths, lyrical legacies, opera heroes and party-starting DJs.

From awesome acoustics to mosh pits and festivals, *The 50 Greatest Musical Places of the World* embraces every music-making genre and seduces readers with journeys to pay homage to pan-African fusion, choral verses and techno beats. From the back-blocks of Nigeria to the exotic locales of Miami and the Caribbean, it showcases 50 places that deserve a place on every music fan's fantasy itinerary, paying homage to a diverse mix of musical shrines, including the obvious, the curious and the obscure: an awe-inspiring musical migration that guarantees to seriously rock your world.

THE 50 GREATEST MUSICAL PLACES OF THE WORLD

UNITED KINGDOM AND IRELAND

MANCHESTER, ENGLAND

It may only be the fifth largest city in the UK in terms of size and population, but Manchester's influence on the UK's culture scene is immense. As an important hub over many generations that has produced some of Europe's finest musical artists across the genres, music has been at the heart of the city for several hundred years. In Elizabethan times, the finest musicians in the city were summoned to the Court Leet to play for royalty and noblemen. Before long, the reputation of Manchester's musical masters was well known in aristocratic circles far and wide. During the classical performances of the early 1800s, the public of Manchester soon became famous for their responsiveness and rapturous applause. This encouraged the composers of Europe, including Liszt and Brahms amongst others, to add the city to their European concert tours. The importance of musical pursuits in Manchester elevated to such a level that the role of music advisor for all Manchester schools was created in 1918. This ensured each school had a choir and orchestra and offered tuition in a variety of instruments. Popular ensembles began to spring up around the city, including the Gentlemen's Glee Club, the Manchester Vocal Society and the Brodsky Quartet. Today Manchester has three symphony orchestras, a chamber orchestra and numerous centres for musical education, including the

Photo: Alan Stanton

prestigious Royal Northern College of Music (RNCM) and Chetham's School of Music.

In 1929 the 250-strong Manchester Children's Choir recorded Henry Purcell's 'Nymphs and Shepherds' and the 'Evening Benediction' from *Hansel and Gretel* with the city's Halle Orchestra at the Free Trade Hall. It followed a year of rehearsals by the 60 boys and 190 girls and was released by Columbia Records, selling a staggering 1 million copies. In 1989, 60 years after it was recorded, EMI awarded the choir a Gold Disc.

Since 1996, Manchester has had an ultra-modern, acoustically-balanced, high-tech 2,500 seat concert venue called the Bridgewater Hall in Lower Mosley Street, where the Halle Orchestra are in residence. Though the old Free Trade Hall has long gone, other historical venues remain, including the RNCM, the Royal Exchange Theatre and a wide variety of halls that are home to many of Northern England's leading brass bands. In England in the early 1990s, the working-class industrialised communities each had a band, usually sponsored by the colliery, steam-powered mill or pit that was the main employer. Manchester has very little pre-industrialised history to speak of, having been powered by the industrial revolution when several of the tall, smoke-spewing chimneys of the area's large-scale cotton mills were visible for miles and miles.

Finally, of course, there is Manchester's richly-endowed pop music scene that played an integral role in every decade from the 1950s to the present day. From the Saints Jazz Band, Derek Atkins' Dixielanders and Smoky City Stompers in the 1950s, Freddie and the Dreamers and Herman's Hermits in the 1960s, 10cc and the Buzzcocks in the 1970s, The Smiths and Joy Division in the 1980s and a whole slew of artists in the 1990s that formed part of the so-called 'Madchester

Scene' such as the Happy Mondays, Stone Roses, Inspiral Carpets, The Charlatans, James and, arguably Manchester's most popular band, Oasis.

Manchester's main pop music venue is the award-winning Manchester Arena: a 21,000-capacity stadium that ranks as Europe's largest. However, many bands prefer to play the more atmospheric venues, such as the Manchester Apollo and Manchester Academy as well as very smallest, the Band on the Wall, the Ruby Lounge and the Bierkeller. As a music city, Manchester is a location to rank alongside New Orleans with its unique sound, high standard of musician-ship and innumerable musical outlets. The city's Factory Records, the legendary oh-so-hip Hacienda nightclub and the old stomping grounds of bands that range from Elbow, The Smiths and Oasis to The Hollies, The Chemical Brothers and the Bee Gees makes Manchester a great place for music-lovers to explore. Manchester tourist offices have a map of the top places to experience the best bands and sounds in the city. There are also musical tours that guide you around the Manchester urban landscape to point out the ordinary city buildings that became iconic once they'd appeared on album covers and posters. Meet the people that inspired Manchester's great musicians, walk in their footsteps and hear first-hand how Manchester has produced more pop-stars per capita of population than any other city in the world.

Unfortunately, at the time of writing, Manchester's finest walking musical tour isn't running due to the sudden death of tour guide Craig Gill – a true stalwart of the city's music scene. As the drummer in Inspiral Carpets, Gill notched up twelve top 40 UK hits, three top ten albums and worked with all of Manchester's most famous music maestros, including Noel Gallagher, Tony Wilson, Johnny Marr, Shaun Ryder,

Mark E Smith, Peter Hook and Dr John Cooper Clarke to name but a few. Gill, who died aged just 44, is survived by the four remaining members of Inspiral Carpets – Graham Lambert, Clint Boon, Martyn Walsh and Steve Holt. A celebration of Gill's life was held at Salford Lads Club: a red brick Manchester venue that famously appeared on The Smiths' 1986 album *The Queen Is Dead*. The club, located in Ordsall, Greater Manchester, has become a place of pilgrimage for Smiths fans ever since the release of the LP. With a capacity for just 200 people, this former youth club is now a much-sought-after venue for intimate, exclusive gigs.

Gill joined the band when he was just 14, and was still touring at the time he died – 30 years after becoming its drummer. Hits by the Inspiral Carpets include 'This Is How It Feels', 'Saturn 5' and 'She Comes In The Fall'. His death shocked the music world with thousands of tributes paid from his contemporaries in bands like Oasis, Stone Roses and Happy Mondays. Gill's highly popular music walks took fans through the city to landmarks synonymous with some of the bands that came out of the Manchester music scene, and his informal, magical personal insight ensured he won 5-star reviews. Gill's relaxed character, easy pace and good humour – coupled with his detailed knowledge of his subject – ensured he always had lots of stories to share.

Morrissey fans should head to the painted iron bridge (where Morrissey decreed, 'Under the iron bridge we kissed, and although I ended up with sore lips' in the song 'Still Ill'), Strangeways (Manchester's high-security male prison designed by Alfred Waterhouse that opened in 1868), his old family house on Kings Road, the Southern Cemetery gates (beyond which many of the city's great and good are buried) and, of course, the Salford Lads Club. Those keen to do a Stone Roses pilgrimage should check out the Hacienda

Night Club (now a block of flats after its entertainment license was revoked in 1997 due to financial mismanagement, theft, drug dealing and violent gangs), Factory Records (the independent label at the heart of the 1990 boom started in 1978 by Tony Wilson and Alan Erasmus – now a club called FAC251) and Eastern Bloc Record Shop on Stevenson Square (where John Squire first heard the funk-laden drumbeat from the James Brown song 'Funky Drummer', that he used so brilliantly on 'Fool's Gold' – the Stone Roses' first UK top ten single). If you are keen to follow in the footsteps of Oasis then be sure to visit the road in which the Gallagher brothers grew up, in truly humble beginnings, before heading to Bonehead's old house in Burnage, where Oasis filmed the music video for their single 'Shaker Maker' in 1993. For added Mancunian ambience, plug one of the great Manc bands into your headphones and pray for grey skies and dark clouds – there is nothing quite like genuine, relentless rainfall for a truly authentic Manchester experience.

Contacts:
Manchester Music Tours
manchestermusictours.com

Visit Manchester
visitmanchester.com

THE ROYAL ALBERT HALL, LONDON, ENGLAND

For over a century, The Prom Season has delighted London's concert goers with a rousing annual classical

Photo: Diliff

music extravaganza of more than 70 concerts over 58 days of music festivities – and more than a few surprises too. An integral part of the classical calendar since 1895, the BBC Proms combines world-class orchestral music and solo performances in the heart of the UK capital, allowing music fans to revel in a world of symphonies, arias and concertos, featuring works from some of history's greatest composers. Yet aside from such luminaries as Elgar, Vivaldi and Beethoven you'll find the innovative, untested and contemporary. In past years, The Proms has showcased British film scores and unknown homespun composers to provide an eclectic mix of chaotic, daring performances – earning a much-deserved reputation as a not-to-be-missed musical jamboree of distinction that champions new music, composers and artists. Each annual Proms Season involves many hundreds of musicians and singers from a wide variety of musical disciplines at concerts at the Royal Albert Hall. However, the highlight of the festival is arguably the world-famous Last Night of the Proms event – a rowdy celebration of over a million people swishing Union Jacks and blowing whistles in patriotic merriment. A perennially popular and grand affair now firmly established as a pinnacle of the UK's music calendar, the Last Night of the Proms offers a chance to revel in an elaborate historic musical tradition of considerable pomp, pageantry and circumstance – an exhilarating, fun-filled finale conducted with energetic aplomb.

Now in its 123rd season, The Proms remains true to its original aim: to present the widest range of music, performed to the highest standards, to large audiences. Since the very first concert in 1895, the tradition has owed much to the brainchild of the event, the impresario Robert Newman, manager of the then newly built Queen's Hall in

London. Newman could see that there was a need to bring symphony orchestras to the general public but deliver them in a less elitist format: inexpensive ticket prices were key as was the informal style of the event. Over time, he developed the project and concluded that it would work best as nightly concerts that eased the audience in via easy stages. His plan involved introducing more popular music at first, gradually raising the standard to incorporate lesser-known and more complex classical and modern music. Each three-hour programme was just one shilling (5p) or a season could be bought for a guinea (£1.05). The series was known as 'Mr Robert Newman's Promenade Concerts' and concert-goers were allowed to eat, drink and smoke during the concerts – though they were asked not to strike matches during the vocal numbers.

Once the crowds had been entertained by some familiar cherry-picked pieces from popular operas, the programme would bring more adventurous pieces to the audience within a wide range of music. This revolutionised how music was showcased to new audiences and allowed young talent to feature alongside leading compositions. Despite sell-out concerts, The Proms ran at a loss. In 1927, the British Broadcasting Corporation (BBC) took over the event and it became a firm fixture in the calendar of the BBC Symphony Orchestra once it was formed in 1930. However, nine years later when Britain declared war on Germany in 1939, the BBC decentralised its Music Department and announced that it was unable to support The Proms. It returned as the sponsor in 1942, by which time the venue was the magnificent Royal Albert Hall, built in 1871.

The Proms have altered over the years to reflect styles and tastes, such as the introduction of a more experimental style of programming in the 1950s and the doubling of the number of bold, new works. In the 1960s, the event expanded its reach to include a great number of international artists as well as concerts by ensembles from non-Western cultures, including India, Thailand, Indonesia and Japan; music for percussion; jazz, gospel and electro-acoustic music; and concerts devised especially for children. The Proms today is a major global music festival on an exciting scale for which the BBC commissions new works each season, offering Proms audiences a chance to hear the latest in musical trends, and creating a unique platform for dozens of contemporary composers. It retains a number of the features introduced in the 1970s, such as a series of Late Night concerts and Pre-Prom Talks. By the end of the 1980s and early 1990s, the programme included more than 70 main Prom concerts every year, ever widening the range of symphonic and operatic music presented.

Don't own a tuxedo, ball-gown or limo? No worries: normal attire or fancy dress, wigs and flags are what lends this unique event its informal atmosphere and allure – especially for the Last Night. This amazing, bizarre, uniquely British event is incredibly popular and tickets for the Last Night are invariably the first to be sold out when the box office opens in mid-May each year. This enthusiastic finale recaps music from each of the main themes for the season, during which the Prommers will behave as impeccably as they normally do, even though they're wearing unusual clothing festooned with Union Jacks and are carrying Union Jack flags. The closing programme is a patriotic finale: 'Land of Hope and Glory' (or Elgar's 'Pomp and Circumstance' March No. 1), the 'Fantasia on British Sea Songs' (including the very popular 'Rule, Britannia!'), and finally 'Auld Lang Syne', 'Jerusalem' and the National Anthem. This is when Prom-goers sway in their seats, rousingly flag-waving, singing along to the music – the atmosphere is amazingly uplifting and everyone is encouraged to join in with whistles and hooters.

Contacts:
The Proms
royalalberthall.com

BBC Live Music Events
bbc.co.uk/events

BBC Philharmonic Orchestra
bbc.co.uk/philharmonic

BARNES, LONDON, ENGLAND

With his flawless skin, pretty face, rose-bud lips and corkscrew, shoulder-length hair, Marc Bolan caused a stir when he first appeared on British TV. Visually, he mixed all-male sex appeal with androgynous rock pizzazz. In canary-yellow satin shirts, a corduroy peaked cap, velvet trousers and strings of coloured beads, London-born Bolan epitomised kooky boho-chic. Sitting cross-legged to play guitar, the songs of this musician-poet-singer-songwriter were more flowery than the usual glam-rock offering. Born plain old Mark Field he had changed his name to Toby Typer after a stint as a catalogue model – a job he owed to his fine, exotic beauty, which in turn owed much to genetics (his father was an Ashkenazi Jew of Russian and Polish descent). He hung around in Soho's coffee bars, mixing in arty circles and falling in love with the rock 'n' roll of Chuck Berry,

Eddie Cochran and Gene Vincent, with his eyelashes coated with mascara and his cheeks dusted with glitter. He rarely left home without six-inch platform boots and his signature purple feather boa. The 1970s mixed up rock 'n' roll with flower power and plenty of psychedelia but, even so, elfin Bolan's daring style cut an outlandish dash. As a musician, Field underwent another change of name to Marc Bolan. In August 1965, he signed to Decca Records and laid down the track 'The Wizard' as his first single, which failed to cause much of a stir. With his band T. Rex he went on to have four UK No.1 hits, including 'Ride A White Swan' and 'Hot Love'. It was a wild, hysterical, weird and hedonistic time and Bolan enjoyed living it to excess.

All that came to a sudden end on 16 September 1977 when he died in the tangled wreck of his purple Mini. It was being driven by his American lover, singer Gloria Jones, when it hit a tree in Barnes, South-west London. Bolan was two weeks from his 30th birthday and they were less than a mile from his home. Texas-born Gloria was a talented soul singer – she recorded the original version of 'Tainted Love' and had worked with Marvin Gaye – when she met Marc. In 1972 he was recording in Germany while she was touring Europe, and he told her how much he liked her music. Both Jones and Bolan were married at the time – he to former publicist June Child, an ex-girlfriend of Pink Floyd's Syd Barrett.

Marc bought a mansion in Richmond, Surrey, and he and Gloria set up home together. Their happiness as a family was complete when she gave birth to their baby boy Rolan. Bolan's eponymous teen music show on Granada (ITV) – Marc – was a hit at teatime in Britain. It showcased new bands (British band The Jam got its big break on Marc) and attracted some megastars, such as Bolan's close friend David Bowie. After Bowie's appearance and the wrap party for the last show in the series, Gloria and Bolan drove home, talking non-stop and in high spirits. Gloria was at the wheel as Bolan had never learned to drive. In the absence of seatbelt laws at that time, neither was strapped into their seat.

Gloria has always denied she was drunk and, though the owner of the restaurant where the couple had dinner that night claimed they had a bottle of wine with their meal, no tests were taken by the police which implicated her. They struck a tree after spinning out of control. Both were thrown through the windscreen: Gloria was found lying on the bonnet and Bolan died instantly after landing on the road. Gloria lay in intensive care for some weeks and awoke to learn that she had lost the love of her life. The accident had also damaged her vocal chords and, as Bolan was still legally married to June when he died, she no longer had a home, any money, or an income. The funeral was a hugely emotional affair, with thousands of Marc Bolan fans sobbing as his swan-topped coffin was carried into the crematorium at Golders Green. Gloria returned to America almost destitute, to live with her parents. David Bowie came to the rescue and arranged to pay for Rolan's education and upkeep. Today she and Rolan have just a handful of mementos of Bolan, including a gold disc, a book of poetry he penned – entitled *The Warlock of Love*, and an autographed tambourine.

Today, 40 years since his death, Marc Bolan's fans continue to maintain a presence at the road that claimed his life. The sycamore tree that their purple Mini 1275GT (registration FOX 661L) hit that fateful night has become one of the world's great, unknown rock shrines. A fastidiously fan-maintained memorial has been erected in Barnes, on Queen's Ride (part of the B306) close to Gipsy Lane and the South Circular. Ever since 16 September

Photo: David Edgar

Photo: David Edgar

IN RESPECTFUL MEMORY OF

MARC BOLAN
30th SEPTEMBER 1947
16th SEPTEMBER 1977

MUSICIAN, WRITER, POET

DONATED BY PERFORMING RIGHT SOCIETY
IN RECOGNITION OF HIS OUTSTANDING
CONTRIBUTION TO BRITISH MUSIC

1977, the accident site has been a place for Bolan pilgrims to converge. Two decades after his death, the Performing Rights Society (PRS) installed a memorial stone at the base of the embankment of the 'Bolan Tree'. A bronze bust of Bolan, paid for exclusively by T-Rex Action Group (TAG) founder Fee Warner, and sculpted by Canadian sculptor Jean Robillard, was unveiled by Rolan. Speed humps are now a feature of Queen's Ride, a relatively quiet road which rises to a blind summit on a railway bridge. TAG has diligently cared for the site and was granted an in perpetuity lease on the land, with ownership and full responsibility for the 'Bolan Tree'. Steps were built to improve access up the muddy embankment to the tree and memorial. In 2005, additional memorial plaques were fitted to the steps to remember other members of T. Rex that have since passed away: Steve Peregrin Took, Mickey Finn, Dino Dines and Steve Currie. Bolan's wife June, who died in 1994, is also recognised for her contribution to his success. Bunches of flowers, potted blooms and brightly-coloured feather boas are draped over kerbstones. In 2007, the site was awarded 'Shrine' status by the English Tourist Board – one of just 113 'Sites of Rock 'n' Roll Importance' in England, joining such iconic musical landmarks as Abbey Road. Scenes of tragic road traffic accidents (RTAs) are turned into temporary shrines all the time, of course. Yet with its black glossy arc-shaped memorial stone, sprouting shrubbery and fine plinth-mounted bronze bust, surrounded by posters, photos and cuttings, this roadside monument to Bolan has stood the test of time. Fans prune the plants, top up the bark chippings and replace the railway sleepers. Fundraising continues for additions such as the spring bulbs that were planted around the capped stump of the sycamore tree when the branches were felled in 2015.

Contacts:
Marc Bolan
marc-bolan.com

T. Rex Action Group (TAG)
mercurymoon.co.uk

Visit London
visitlondon.com

HANDEL AND HENDRIX HOUSE, LONDON, ENGLAND

In one street in the west end of London, two neighbouring houses share an extraordinary musical heritage as the former homes of history-changing virtuosos. One, was where George Frideric Handel lived, a composer who gained fame at the Royal Academy of Music in England; the other was home to probably the biggest rock legend in music history, the guitar hero Jimi Hendrix.

Hendrix enjoyed living in Brook Street, in the heart of London, welcoming the freedom it offered. He would walk from the flat to pop into HMV and flick through its shelves of vinyl. Legendary venues like the Marquee and the Speakeasy were also close by. With his girlfriend Kathy Etchingham, he would go out to the local Indian restaurant: there were no paparazzi to bother him and he was rarely asked for autographs over his pile of poppadoms. Hendrix and Etchingham were together for three years, and he once claimed that she was 'my past girlfriend, my present

Photo: Simon Harriyott

girlfriend and probably my future girlfriend; my mother, my sister and all that bit. My Yoko Ono'. He wrote 'Foxy Lady', 'Gypsy Eyes' and 'The Wind Cries Mary' for her and the couple were inseparable: she booked the recording studios and watched as he auditioned his band. According to Etchingham, Hendrix was fundamentally a sensitive and shy guy.

Born in America, Jimi Hendrix grew up in Seattle where he was shunted between foster parents and relatives of his dead, alcoholic mother. He spent the last four years of his life in London – one of his happiest periods – describing Brook Street as 'the only home I ever had'. He was discovered playing in a Greenwich Village coffee house by the Animals' bassist Chas Chandler, who declared him 'the greatest guitarist ever'. Chandler brought him to London, where Hendrix arrived with a white Fender Stratocaster guitar, some hair curlers and a tube of spot cream as luggage. On his first night out on the town, he met Etchingham whilst performing at the Scotch of St James's nightclub. He had formed a trio, the Jimi Hendrix Experience, and went on to have hits with 'Hey Joe' and 'Purple Haze'. Kathy gave up her job as a hairdresser and found the flat in the Evening Standard newspaper for a rent of £30 a week. Hendrix loved it, especially when he learned that the German composer Handel had lived next door for 36 years. After rushing out to buy a copy of 'Messiah', Handel's superlative Easter oratorio, he claimed to have seen the composer's ghost disappearing into a wall, describing him as looking like 'an old guy in a night shirt and grey pigtail'.

Stories that Etchingham has shared about her time with Hendrix conjure up a conservative domestic scene, quite unlike the hedonistic headlines that described his demons after his premature death. They'd go shopping, enjoy quiet time out of the limelight drinking tea and watching *Coronation Street* (Hendrix was a great Ena Sharples fan), and would go ice skating in Bayswater Road. Sure, they'd also party until breakfast and sleep until dusk too – it was the height of the Swinging Sixties in London. Paid for by Hendrix's management company in Gerrard Street, their Brook Street home was open to anyone and visiting musicians would often knock on the flat door – Keith Moon and Keith Richards would often pop by, sitting on the end of the bed in the absence of chairs. But it wasn't all domestic bliss. Hendrix wasn't faithful, inventing the term 'Band Aids' for the groupies that hung on his arm, and 'The Wind Cries Mary' (Etchingham's middle name is Mary), was written after Kathy hit him with a frying pan. Despite his dalliances, Hendrix was prone to extreme jealousy when his girlfriend attracted male attention. With his army jacket, Afro hair and flowery shirts, the black American was like nothing London had seen before – women were enthralled; men admiring.

Hendrix died on 18 September 1970, of an overdose, aged just 27, after his occasional glass of Mateus rosé and celebratory whisky and coke had escalated to regular use of cocaine, LSD and finally heroin. Hendrix and Etchingham had split up by then because she couldn't cope with the hedonistic rock 'n' roll lifestyle – he was devastated and moved into the Cumberland Hotel near Marble Arch. She saw him in Kensington Market the day he died – haggard and prematurely grey. Later that night, in the company of German former skating champion Monika Dannemann in Kensington's Samarkand Hotel, Hendrix is believed to have inadvertently overdosed on sleeping pills mixed with booze and choked on his own vomit – though his death is still an open verdict. Claims of something more sinister continue to be made today, and Etchingham spent three years investigating the circumstances of Hendrix's death in the 1990s. Dannemann lost a libel case against her, committing suicide 48 hours later in her fume-filled Mercedes. Theories surrounding the time and cause of death have become the stuff of legends. The fans he had made through his intense period of playing in London clubs, as well as venues across the UK were distraught at his untimely passing. Hendrix, who once confided that his father used to beat him 'senseless' for trying to learn the guitar by putting string on a broom, had made the big time and had headlined at the Royal Albert Hall.

George Frideric Handel, who lived at neighbouring 25 Brook Street for 36 years, wrote many of his greatest works there, including the 'Messiah'. Both properties are now owned by the Handel House Trust, which has been using Hendrix's former home as an office, only opening it occasionally to the public. Acknowledging that few streets in the world could claim such a concentration of musical genius, the trust decided to open Jimi Hendrix's flat as a permanent attraction in 2016, following painstaking research into the building and Hendrix's circle of friends and acquaintances to understand exactly how it looked when he lived there. At the heart of the Hendrix flat is the main living room where he spent many hours of writing and countless jam sessions with visiting musicians. He slept here, entertained here and played records so loudly his two giant speakers kept breaking. The level of detail used to recreate the flat is remarkable, right down to Hendrix's two telephones – one old-school black Bakelite, one modishly angular – on the floor and the scallop shell ashtray on the bedside table. The bed, draped in hippy-ish fabrics under a canopy of embroidered silks, is scattered with brightly-coloured cushions. Kathy Etchingham, who now lives in Australia, was a consultant on the replication project – insisting Hendrix was fastidiously tidy and obsessively neat, after a spell in the army. The flat has a modish pink bathroom suite and a kitchen that was barely used as the couple relied on 'room service' from Mr Love's, the restaurant downstairs. Some beautiful black and white photographs snapped for *Melody Maker* in January 1969 have also been used to help recreate the room. There is also a wall of album covers, and an index of the music played on the Bang & Olufsen turntable, including records by Acker Bilk, the Beatles, the Band, Ravi Shankar and Bob Dylan – whose track 'Like a Rolling Stone', Hendrix said, 'made me feel that I wasn't the only one who'd ever felt so low'. In the corner of the room there stands the Epiphone FT79 acoustic guitar, which the rock star bought in New York at the end of his first US tour. A peacock screen and a pile of old newspapers also help to transport visitors back to the '60s.

On 14 September 1997, Hendrix's old flat at 23 Brook Street was chosen for an English Heritage blue plaque commemorating his life and work. It is the only officially recognised Hendrix residence in the world. London has become an important destination for rock pilgrims and a number of award-winning tours visit rock's monumental landmarks. These include places featured on album covers, stars' homes, recording studios, gig sites, clubs and video and film locations – the places that inspired the lyrics and the bands. Some of the most important sites for rock pilgrimages include the London homes of the Beatles, the Apple offices (the Beatles' own record label) and all the other key Fab Four-related places. Other tours focus on the Rolling Stones, Led Zeppelin, Queen, The Clash, The Who,

The Kinks, David Bowie, The Sex Pistols, Pink Floyd, Eric Clapton, Coldplay, Blur and Amy Winehouse.

Contacts:
Handel-Hendrix Museum
handelhendrix.org

Rock and Trips
rockandtrips.co.uk

London Rock Tours
londonrocktour.com

London Rock Walks
londonrockwalks.com

EISTEDDFOD FESTIVAL, WALES

The lilting timbre and mellow tone of the Welsh voice choir is musical shorthand for Wales and the choral tradition holds a special place in the emblematic culture of the Valleys. In the working class industrial communities of the Welsh heartlands, male voice choirs have long been a feature, especially in the south of the country. Throughout the written history of Wales, the propensity for gathering men in large numbers has been chronicled – in the coal mines, in the pub, at the rugby and in song. In the 1950s, Welsh rugby captain Cliff Morgan said that the singing at matches put a yard on every stride, and 20 yards on every kick. What made the music-making of Wales become so iconic lies in the incredible resonance of the voices working in harmony. Lyrics and their respective parts are learnt by heart, with the choir's attention focused solely on the conductor – not written scores. Traditional songs and hymns remain the bedrock of the Welsh male voice choir repertoire, with the modern addition of some light opera and classic pop standards. A stirring rendition of 'Men of Harlech' – a song about Owain Glyndwr's defence of Cambria from English invaders is a show-stopping favourite with audiences throughout Wales.

Rock and pop icons of Wales – from Tom Jones, Catatonia to Stereophonics – have performed with male voice choirs (*côr meibion* as the male-voice choir tradition is known in Welsh) as an aural and visual mark of identity of their homeland. There is joy, camaraderie, high spirits and nostalgia in singing as well as the strong connection it maintains with national identity and pride. Though Wales doesn't quite have a male voice choir on each street corner, it isn't uncommon for every community – city, town or village – to have an age-old choral tradition. The congregational vocal style: singing songs not in unison but in parts, so that numerous songs and a variety of choral layers sing at different intervals; seems to date back to the 12th century at least. Until the reformation, song schools in the Roman church tradition seem to have flourished, but from Tudor times onwards – particularly with the exodus of musicians from Wales to the English court – church music had a very lean time of it. Hymns, introduced during the rise of non-conformity in the 18th century, were adapted to melodies derived from olden Welsh folk tunes. They soon formed part of weekly Sunday worship when congregations were part-singing with joyous relish from the pews. Singing in parts created great rivalries between the neighbouring voice choirs and the choral works by hymn-

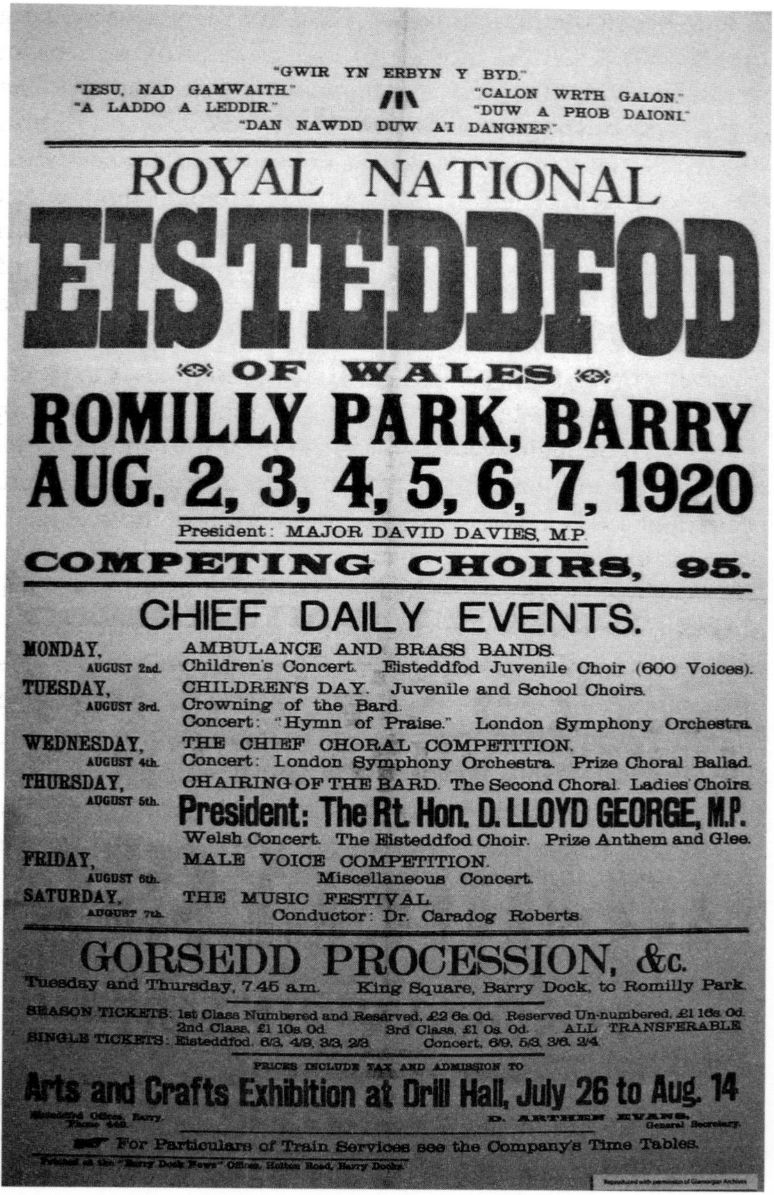

Photo: Rhyswynne

writers Joseph Parry, David Evans and David Jenkins were in high demand.

Today, male voice choirs remain very much 'comrades in arms' with the rehearsal, the performance and the post-song social gathering all very much part of the bond. In the past, the average age of a choir member was younger: reflecting the life expectancy of miners and steel workers. Today around 65 per cent of the 10,000 Welsh male choristers are aged over 55. The sizes of the choirs have changed too, with most consisting of around 50 men – far smaller than the gigantic choral brotherhoods of old. Yet the repertoire of these smaller choirs – with their lungs puffed out booming tenor and bass notes – continues to provide the soundtrack to everything from the chapel, to the rugby field, to the rowdy pub sing-along. The oldest male voice choir – a 68-strong group from Gwent, the Pontnewydd Male Voice Choir – are flag-wavers for longevity, clocking up more than 110 years of musical tradition and doing much to raise the profile of Welsh choirs everywhere. These days almost none are miners, steelworkers or quarrymen – those industries have mainly died out. Yet choir members are still held in high regard: on the passing of elders, local newspapers devote full-page tributes to those singers recently deceased. The tenderness, warmth and sharing nature of song may seem at odds with trademark Welsh man's gruff machismo but the obvious passion for song, and for their brethren, says 'we love Wales, there's no place like home'.

Shaped by the last Ice Age, some 10,000 years ago, Wales' storied terrain is rich in ragged mountains, sparkling natural lakes (around 400 at last count), fish-filled rivers and waterfalls. Resplendent beaches, coves and coastal plains are home to hundreds of avian, floral and plant species. And despite being a small country, (20,782 sq kms

(8,024 sq miles)) of just 3 million people, Wales has a trio of scenic national parks: the Pembrokeshire coast, Snowdonia and Brecon Beacons. Speciality foods, a distinctive Celtic language and a slew of fascinating legends, cultures, myths and traditions are part of the Welsh landscape and its history.

Visitors in Wales keen to discover the sound of its male voice choirs will find innumerable opportunities to watch a performance, attend a concert or simply join a rehearsal. For larger all-male choral festivals, visit the Welsh Association of Male Choirs website: welshassocmalechoirs.co.uk – you'll find the locations and contact details for all of the 80 member choirs plus a list of upcoming events. Wales is also proud of its *eisteddfod*: a Welsh festival of music, literature and performance that takes place country-wide – the largest is the National Eisteddfod in Anglesey, which takes place in the first week of August each year. The site of the festival travels from place to place, alternating between North and South Wales, and attracts around 150,000 visitors and a staggering 6,000 music and dance competitors each year.

The history of the Eisteddfod in Wales can be traced back to 1176 with the modern history of the organisation staging a festival yearly since 1864, other than when it was postponed in 1914 on the outbreak of the Second World War. Most of Wales' leading singers and musicians have competed at the Eisteddfod, as well as writers and poets. Tickets go on sale on 1 April every year, see: eisteddfod.org.uk.

Contacts:
Visit Wales
visitwales.com

Association of Welsh Male Voice Choirs
welshassocmalechoirs.co.uk

MACHYNLLETH, WALES

When Led Zeppelin's greatest landmarks were added to Google Maps and Google Earth a few years ago there was a notable swell in the number of Led-Zep pilgrims beating a path to their door. Not that they necessarily need to travel, as fans can now use Google to tour virtually around sites that are pivotal in the group's history. For the fans of Led Zeppelin are a phenomenal breed: fiercely loyal and utterly devoted. When the box office opened for the reunion gig in 2007, Led Zeppelin's fans snapped up every ticket in less than a couple of hours. It's not just tickets that are gold dust: a rare vintage Zep t-shirt from a 1979 Knebworth Park gig sold for $10,000 at auction in 2011. And when Led Zeppelin's back catalogue was remastered, the fans propelled the first three albums back into the charts a week after they were re-released. Yep, just like the hit song, the fans show their idols 'A Whole Lotta Love'.

Each member of Led Zeppelin had a formidable reputation as a session musician before teaming up to form the band. As a result, when it came to signing their first album deal with Atlantic, they knew the ropes and wangled an unprecedented $20,000 advance, as well as almost full publishing rights to their music. It wasn't long before Led Zeppelin were making a lot of money and had plenty of cash sloshing about for gadgets and perks. Zeppelin pioneered some pretty huge sonic breakthroughs in rock music, such as the revolutionary reverse echo Jimmy Page often used. In typical style, Page downplayed the whole thing: 'I was just in the studio twisting knobs,' he once told *Rolling Stone*. They spent plenty of money on

Photo: Celtici

41

guitars plural, with one axe not enough for Page, who was a famous early adopter of Gibson's double-necked EDS-1275 model – voted the coolest guitar in rock in a 2012 poll. What the Beatles were to the '60s, Led Zeppelin were to the '70s: a band so successful and innovative that they defined music for an entire generation. They stuck to their guns, refusing to release singles off their albums, and ushered in the era of album rock. Despite this, Led Zep records received plenty of radio airtime, proving that their type of arena rock didn't need to conform to the three-minute format. Record company nil: Led Zep, one. The band pushed hard to play in ever-larger stadiums and ticket sales continued to skyrocket. By 1973, Zeppelin had their own custom plane, the Starship. It was the envy of the rock world with a bar with a keyboard organ built in, a video library and shower room. Costing $30,000 to lease, it was hired by Deep Purple, the Rolling Stones and Peter Frampton. But it was Led Zeppelin who created the rock band blueprint for hedonism – at home and abroad. The band's partying is a thing of legend and there are dozens of stories about crazy nights of girls, drink and drugs. Once, they rented six floors of the Andaz West Hollywood Hotel in LA and hosted a drug-fuelled orgy while drummer John Bonham rode a motorbike down hotel corridors. Other tales aren't as tame.

From the start Led Zeppelin lived life large, creating unapologetically big music and yielding songs that made a massive sound from the band as a whole. Everything worked, brilliantly: John Bonham's apocalyptic drumming, Robert Plant's wailing, Jimmy Page's rip-roaring guitar solos, and even John Paul Jones's funky bass grooves. Every individual member of the band is considered the greatest in their field. Together, they have sold over 200 million albums worldwide

– an elite category reserved for the greatest artists ever. They are adored by fans and respected by famous musicians with the long list of bands that cite Led Zeppelin as an influence, including Metallica, Madonna, Red Hot Chili Peppers, Alice Cooper and Beastie Boys to name a few. They shifted the psychedelic era of the 1960s into to the feral, sexually driven rock of the 1970s. Artistic, masculine, sexy and cool: Led Zeppelin also had a major impact on fashion with everyone keen to give off that hot, titanic roar. The vibe echoed the loud, riff-heavy palpable urgency of the records – the music was laced with desire, rich in depth and physical yearning. Everywhere they played, Led Zeppelin left legends of excess along the way.

Led Zeppelin's sledgehammer beat, as solid as granite, softened against the melody of the folk refrains and the band's 'Stairway to Heaven', an eight-minute epic became the most played song in the history of album-oriented radio, yet was never released as a single. Page's guitar style drew heavily on the blues and he wove funk beats and reggae pulses into thunderous rock tracks. He experimented freely, becoming a master of distortion, feedback and reverberation. Yet he harnessed the out-and-out noise so that it was more than screaming metal and would tease his rock riffs with a delicate, feather-light touch. Touring relentlessly for years and producing albums that broke all records became the pace of the band. They retreated for a while in 1977, cancelling a US tour when Robert Plant's five-year-old son died from a lung infection. Plant was utterly distraught, and the anguish caused him to consider turning his back on music for a career in teaching. However, Led Zeppelin resurfaced after eighteen months in 1979, releasing the much-delayed eighth studio album, *In Through The Out Door*. It entered the charts at number one in both America and England – and in May 1980 the band embarked on what was to be their last European tour. Later that year, in September, whilst the band prepared itself for an American tour, John Bonham was found dead, in bed at Page's home. Having binged on booze and vomited, Bonham had died of asphyxiation.

The band disbanded, broken-hearted, and began working on solo projects. In 1985, the remaining members of Led Zeppelin reunited for Live Aid, with drummers Phil Collins and Tony Thompson on stage. For Atlantic's 25th anniversary concert in 1988, the band re-formed again, this time with John Bonham's son Jason. In 1989 and 1992 remastered versions of records became the fastest selling box-sets of all time. Page and Plant reunited to record an acoustic segment for MTV Unplugged in 1994. The following year, they played together on a series of international tour dates which led to an all-new studio recording in 1998 – disappointingly, the album wasn't a massive hit anywhere other than America. However in 2006, ecstatic Led Zep fans finally got the news they had long awaited – a full reunion of the surviving members of the band, with Jason Bonham filling the role of his father on drums. The historic concert took place in 2007 at London's O2 with the entire set filmed and recorded. It was finally released under the title *Celebration Day* in the autumn of 2012.

Since then, Page has become the group's unofficial archivist, painstakingly sifting through vintage Zeppelin material for re-release. The result is a massive back catalogue of work containing newly remastered versions of their albums, a project that hit the shelves in 2014, in CD, high-resolution downloads and vinyl, with additional deluxe editions of previously unreleased material from the vaults. In 2016 the band re-released *The Complete BBC*

Sessions, including eight previously unreleased recordings.

Led Zeppelin's landmarks on Google Earth and Google Maps include the Olympic Cinema in Barnes – an early 20th-century building that was once the go-to recording studio for Led Zeppelin and other rock groups, which since 2013 has been a two-screen movie theatre. Jimmy Page's Scottish mansion Boleskine House is another plot on the map, as is the state-of-the-art O2 Arena on the Greenwich peninsula in South-east London, and drummer John Bonham's grave in the West Midlands town of Rushock. There are more Led Zeppelin connections in Machynlleth in rural Wales, including a ramshackle cottage owned by Robert Plant in Bron-Yr-Aur above Dyfi Bridge. It was here that the band escaped to in May 1970 after a gruelling fifteen-month tour for some peace and quiet. Page and Plant wrote many of the songs that appear on the *Led Zeppelin III* album here as well as the 'Bron-yr-Aur' track on the *Physical Graffiti* album. In fact the cottage is even thanked on the sleeve notes of *Led Zeppelin III*. Page and Plant are believed to have used the cottage as a writing base again in 1994 ahead of the MTV Unplugged session. With no electricity or mains water, they were forced to trek down to the Glyndwr Hotel in Machynlleth for a weekly bath. Jimmy Page once lived on the River Thames in a wooden houseboat and the riverside walks around the mooring in Pangbourne are surrounded by some scenic countryside. Another attraction popular with the most devoted of fans is Guildford University – where the band's first UK gig was played.

Contacts:
Led Zeppelin
ledzeppelin.com

Visit Britain
visitbritain.com

London Rock Tours
londonrocktours.com

GLASGOW AND STIRLING, SCOTLAND

It is a sound that is distinctly Scottish, despite it being an instrument that is found in other parts of the world. Bagpipes, the pressure-squeezed bag with reed pipes that is carried under the player's arm, signify a toe-tapping tune, a funeral procession, a jovial dance and a hearty sing-a-long. Bagpipe music reverberates around Scotland – in cities, rural communities and on civil occasions. Street pipers blast the pipes at public events while to those in mourning, the gentle sound of a solitary bagpipe can carry poignant memories into the echoes of the churchyard.

The first use of bagpipes can be traced back to pre-medieval times as far back as 1,300 BC. Nero of the Roman Empire played the pipes and extolled the virtues of bagpipe music, and history suggests that marching legions were accompanied by piping. Later, wandering shepherds would play forlorn pipe tunes as they tended to their flocks, reflecting the emotions of hours alone. Bagpipes are enshrined in Scottish folklore, yet they are not exclusively found there and are also common to the Middle East, Spanish-speaking countries and parts of Eastern Europe. A convoluted history thrust the traditional Scottish bagpipes (officially called Great Highland) into battle at Bannockburn in 1314 and it is still traditional in ceremonial terms for a Scottish regiment to be accompanied by a piper. They found their footing in Scotland in the 1700s, when they became more than just a part of Scottish myth and legend, and began to play a clear role in community, society and ritual. Today the Scots value their bagpipes as an integral part of their national identity: to them the Great Highland bagpipe, with its three drones, familiar tone and character, is as Scottish as tartan.

During the 14th and 15th centuries, Celtic customs received a boost as the importance of pipes was furthered by Robert the Bruce's son King David II and King James I of Scotland (1394–1437). Both were patrons of the bagpipe and there is evidence that so too was James IV (1488–1513). Today, Queen Elizabeth II retains a personal piper whose refrain awakens her each morning, such are the lifelong ties that bind her to a much-favoured part of her kingdom: a country that is much more than just a quarter of the United Kingdom – it's a full-blooded part of her heart.

The pipes have incited warriors to battle, roused armies and been fostered by Scotland's oldest clans and leading families. Individual tunes differ greatly from one another but conform to rules of composition and follow a definite plan. A syllabic notation is used to preserve the music and pass it on to new pupils. The MacCrimmons, a clan of hereditary pipers, founded a famous piping school at Boreraig in Vaternish, Skye in the 16th century and schooled a dynasty of great pipers. Tunes that survive from the earliest times consist of marches and battle-tunes, salutes, gatherings and laments. Considered a war instrument since the 16th century, the battle of Culloden in 1746 signified a time when bagpipe players were considered combatant in the eyes of the law, as no regiment marched without a piper. Since then bagpipes have had strong military associations in the British

Army where the Pipe Major is a position of honour. It is the piper's duty is to rouse his cold, frightened and demoralised comrades out of the trenches and into action. Over 1,000 pipers fell during the First World War and the pipes came to represent bravery, strength, courage and heroism.

Visitors to modern Scotland will still encounter the iconic sounds of the bagpipes during street parades, on town squares, at Highland games, at gigs, music events and Gaelic ceremonies, and during traditional Scottish festivities. Many museums and castles have pipes amongst their collections with the most comprehensive permanent exhibition found at the National Piping Centre in Glasgow where the patron is HRH Prince Charles. A fascinating narrative transports visitors across more than 300 years of bagpipe history from its military role and place within nobility to its place in modern-day society. As the home of the oldest surviving chanter of the Highland bagpipe anywhere in the world, the museum is a Centre of Excellence for pipe training. Next door, there is a bagpipe shop where instruments, reeds, music and traditional Highland wear (tartan kilts, pure-wool socks, leather shoes and quilted woollen jackets) are sold, together with an academy that trains bagpipers to a high level of expertise. A range of courses and workshops offer novices a chance to get acquainted with this iconic musical instrument.

There is also a much-respected bagpipe maker in Stirling where handmade pipes and accessories are crafted in a small family-owned workshop. Stirling Bagpipes is run by Alan Waldron, who makes high quality Highland bagpipes as well as smallpipes and borderpipes to both standard and bespoke designs. He also has an enviable collection of antique bagpipes of famous makes available for purchase. Waldron once worked for Garvie Bagpipes, a leading firm

Photo: Dalbera

of Scottish bagpipe makers based in Edinburgh, where he mastered the art of reed making, bellow making, lathe work and tuning. Visitors can also learn more about all things piping at the much-celebrated Piping Live – Glasgow's epic, week-long bagpipe festival which takes place in August each year. With bagpipe demonstrations and performances morning, noon and night, the venues at Piping Live are as varied as the concerts: from workshops to master classes and street performances. The World Pipe Band Championships also takes place during the festival.

Contacts:
National Piping Centre
thepipingcentre.co.uk

Piping Live
pipinglive.co.uk

Scottish Tourism
visitscotland.com/see-do/events/

EUROPE

MADRID, SPAIN

Madrid's flamenco scene is firmly entrenched in the city's cobblestoned old quarter where daylight hours are a relaxed affair of pigeon-scattered plazas, pavement cafés and snoozing street-corner traders. After dark, the city bursts into life as restaurants and bars fill and music flows as freely as the wine – vibrant, intense and exciting. Cosy bars, cafés and *terrazas* form the heart of Old Madrid's spirit, where conversation and dance are both engaged in, always with passion – but rarely without liquid accompaniment. People flow in and out of the *tabernas* (traditional style taverns), *cervecerías* (speciality beer bars), *cocterlerías* (cocktail bars) and *bares de copas* (serving speciality spirits) through unassuming, dimly lit doorways. Late at night, the city's side-street *tablaos* (establishments with a stage used for flamenco performances) throw open their doors to an eager audience keen to ignite the shadows with the fiery passion of dance. Stunning interiors adorned with traditional tile-work, boldly painted ceramic murals, scrubbed wooden floors and lime-washed walls evoke the bygone aura of another age. *Madrileños* joke that the day begins at 10pm when the lights dim, clubs open and crowds swell into the city – an exaggeration, but almost true. Traditional flamenco has its time now, stirring Madrid with an intoxicating energy of whirling colour and the firecracker clack sound of heels on tile.

Gypsy-originated flamenco rejects formality, preferring the freedom of improvised movements to mirror the mood of the moment in great exuberance and intensity. Young and old radiate to such venues as Corral de la Morería, Café de Chinitas, Torres Bermejas and Taberna Casa Patas, where flamenco's finest performers include Chaquetón, Remedios Amaya, Chano Lobato and La Niña Pastori – to name but a few. A month-long Festival Flamenco Caja Madrid at the Albéniz Theater (c/Paz) showcases the best in flamenco. Short, sharp claps and soulful cries rise above the music with a resonance that burrows deep into the night-time still.

A dance genre characterised by rapid passages and audible footwork, flamenco is thought to derive from the Arabic

Photo: Kalaiarasy

music traditions of Moorish times. Strumming guitars follow the rhythms as dancers take to the floor, chins perfectly poised and arms aloft. As the so-called 'dance of the people' flamenco welcomes visitor applause and participation, from encouraging claps and stamps to shouts and shrieks. The skill is to simply allow your body to yield to the rhythm (the *compás*) and let it feel the musical pulse rather than mechanically count the beats. Watch the masters as they close their eyes and surrender to the escalating syncopated tempo: the raw emotion is palpable as the music emits the power of lust, joy, passion and mournful lament.

One of Madrid's most famous flamenco musicians was guitar virtuoso Ramón Montoya, one of the earliest flamenco superstars, born in the city in 1880. Madrid adored Montoya's unique singing and guitar style, which soon became his trademark throughout flamenco circles across Spain. Today you'll hear his musical imprint in the artistry of many of the Madrid flamenco artists that entertain the circuit – even some 50 years after his death. Ramón Montoya is honoured in almost all of the city's flamenco joints, often in a fine set of black and white prints on the wall. He introduced the open D tuning, lowering the 6th string by one tone to give the flamenco guitar two open 4th and 6th strings in D. He also used a third string tuning to F sharp, tuning the strings from bass to treble in D, A, D, F-sharp, B and E. His nephew Carlos Montoya went on to achieve international acclaim for his solo flamenco instrumentals.

When Ramón Montoya died in Madrid in 1949 he received the style of funeral usually reserved for noblemen and royalty. During his lifetime, he witnessed the popularity of flamenco spread nationwide, from its roots in the plazas in small towns in the southern reaches of Spain to the bright lights and bustle of the capital. Once people started to travel, the energy, colour and beauty of flamenco journeyed too with many famous artists crossing Spain for the first time to perform. Initially, there was a rivalry for the heart of flamenco between Madrid and the countryside. However, today flamenco purists from Andalusia are more accepting of Madrid's glitzy scene. The popular quote says: 'Flamenco was born in Andalusia, but is performed in Madrid' – an expression that helps us understand the modern role of the city in flamenco's development. Today many thousands of flamenco-lovers from southern Spain flock to the city each year to patronise the best venues and shows.

Unlike the rural tradition of Andalusia, flamenco in the metropolis is a year-round affair with the oldest venue, the Corral de la Moreria, first staging a show in 1956. There isn't much sign of life here until after midnight and many of the performances begin with one of Madrid's celebrity flamenco A-list holding informal chats with fans, signing albums and discussing touring plans, introducing the history of flamenco art in Spain or pouring special sherry to accompany the music. (Corral de la Moreria, Calle de la Moreria tel: +34 913 65 11 37). Events centre around a beautifully-prepared dinner in Casa Patas: a tavern-style eatery set around the floor on which the flamenco show takes place. As a well-respected flamenco school and charity, the dinner and show help to raise funds for the venue (Casa Patas, Calle de los Canizares tel: +34 913 69 04 96). The prestigious Torres Bermejas has hosted many of Spain's finest flamenco artists and counts the queen of Spain, other members of Spanish nobility and TV stars amongst its fans. Since it opened in 1960, it has wowed audiences with its stunning décor which draws on the Granada's Alhambra in its tones, hues and designs (Torrese Bermejas, Calle Mesoneros Romanos, tel: +34 915 32 33 22). Another much-acclaimed venue is Caramomo, a flamenco foundation dedicated to promoting the genre across the world that was polled 'Best in Madrid' by *The New York Times*. Located right in the melée of Puerta del Sol, it first invited musicians to play when it opened in 1994 and now attracts one of the biggest crowds in the capital, just a short stroll from the metro station. (Cardamom, Calle Ecegaray, tel: +34 918 05 10 38). Decorated in rustic Andalusian style, Café de Chinitas oozes with the charm of southern Spain. Food is central to the experience here and the menu is packed with home-cooked tastes of Cordoba, Malaga and Seville. Find it in a handsome 18th-century palace, near Gran Via in the heart of the city – two 90-minute shows each day (except Sunday) sell out fast so be sure to pre-book. (Café de Chinitas, Calle Torija, tel: +34 915 47 15 02). Another atmospheric venue lauded by the critic is Las Tablas, one of the newest names in flamenco in the capital at around a decade old. Like Café de Chinitas, it stages two shows each day (at 8pm and 10pm). Choose from tickets that come as entry only, with tapas or with dinner – the menu includes vegetarian options, a rarity in Madrid (Las Tablas, Plaza Espana tel: +34 91 54 20 520).

A number of companies run flamenco tours of Madrid, including musical lessons and walks through flamenco neighbourhoods. One of the best private tour operators is Yolanda Martín whose knowledge of flamenco goes beyond the norm, ensuring you don't just enjoy listening to world-class singers and guitarists, you'll actually understand the origins, sentiments and motivation of the music and culture.

Contacts:
Yolanda Martín
theflamencoguide.com

Ogo Tours
ogotours.com

Madrid Tourist Board
esmadrid.com

PARIS, FRANCE

Since his untimely passing in 1971 in a Parisian apartment, the death of Jim Morrison has remained one of rock music's most tantalising mysteries. Speculation continues to this day as to exactly how the charismatic frontman of The Doors died, including suggestions he was killed by a heroin overdose in the toilets of a nightclub and that drug dealers moved his body in a cover-up. Officially, according to the death certificate anyway, Morrison died in the bath, of 'natural causes' – an explanation that will always attract conspiracy theorists. Whatever the truth, his death at 27 saw him join the legendary '27 Club' – a mythical club of iconic musicians that have died at age 27 as a result of drugs, drink, suicide or violent means. Morrison's fellow members include Brian Jones, Jimi Hendrix, Janis Joplin, Kurt Kobain and, most recently, Amy Winehouse.

As one of the world's most widely recognisable stars, Jim Morrison enjoyed the relative anonymity that Paris offered, arriving in the French capital in March 1971. After huge hits such as 'Break on Through' and 'Light My Fire', he had just finished recording what was to become The Doors' most popular album, *LA Woman*. His wild-man lifestyle revolved around alcohol and drugs and he soon became a regular

Photo: Axel301

at the Rock 'n' Roll Circus, a basement club frequented by the Beatles, the Rolling Stones, Pink Floyd, Eric Clapton and Jimi Hendrix. It attracted a madcap arty crowd and featured trapeze artists and, on one memorable occasion, a live tiger and monkeys from a nearby circus. At around 1am on 3 July 1971, Morrison joined around 500 club-goers, including 24-year-old British siren Marianne Faithfull who had recently split up with Mick Jagger. He drank from a bottle of vodka and ordered numerous beers and looked every inch the cool, handsome, rugged Californian rock god. Accounts vary of what transpired in the wee small hours, but Morrison's lifeless body was discovered in his apartment across the river in Rue Beautreillis just a few hours later. Incredibly, no proper investigation into his death was carried out by the French authorities. A doctor signed off Morrison's demise as 'death from natural causes' and ruled that no autopsy was required, as there was 'no evidence of foul play'. The official death report, still filed at Paris town hall today, has been used to quash countless conspiracy theories in the last three-and-a-half decades, ranging from security agency plots to theories that Morrison faked his own death to escape the trappings of fame. The Parisian medic who filed the death report pointed out that Morrison had been unwell before he left America with respiratory complaints, stomach ulcers and other ailments linked to his escalating substance abuse.

Today legions of super-fans own all 22 Doors albums, including anniversary specials, box sets, live recordings and a number of gold-dust rarities. They travel to Paris to sightsee, sure – but not the French architecture, world famous paintings and the Eiffel Tower. No. They arrive to visit one of the least-talked about, most-visited places in Paris – Jim Morrison's grave. The Père-Lachaise Cemetery is hidden away in the 20th arrondissement, with Morrison's body laid to rest amongst the remains of great French writers, philosophers, war heroes, champions and artists. His tombstone is immediately obvious: notable not for its size or grandeur but for flowers, music paraphernalia, fan letters and graveside tourists around it.

Also laid to rest in this leafy, tree-lined city space, with its tranquil pathways and its verdant glades, are Oscar Wilde, classical composer Chopin, American writer Gertrude Stein, French artist Géricault, Édith Piaf, and visionary architect George-Eugène Haussmann – the creative talent behind Paris as you see it today. At just a few minutes from the noisy, pulsating heart of the French capital it feels celestial, surreal and overwhelming to consider the stories buried beneath your feet. In the days before his death, Morrison had been focused on his writing and his beautiful poetic lyrics freely flowed. Fittingly he has been laid to rest in the cemetery's 'Poets' Corner' among men that he once named as great influences such as French poets Arthur Rimbaud and Charles Baudelaire.

Around two to three hundred fans visit Jim Morrison's grave in the Père-Lachaise Cemetery on an ordinary day – it is significantly more on anniversaries. As many as 20,000 gathered for the 30th anniversary of his death – enough to bring the police out in force. CCTV monitors the tombstone, which has been the focal point for graffiti in the past. Once the police had to disperse fans with tear gas after the crowds became rowdy – an ironic scene in which thousands of young people inspired by Morrison's rebelliousness were turned away at the cemetery gates. It transpired that rumours had circulated that the lease on Morrison's grave plot was due to expire and the French authorities were planning to exhume his body. It stirred up bad feeling and the mood turned ugly, even though the speculation turned out to be unfounded.

The cemetery is easy to find from the tree-lined boulevard of Ménilmontant and is entered via the gate at Ave du Boulevard and Ave du Principale. Maps are sold detailing the location of famous graves to help the unfamiliar first-time visitor wandering around all the many headstones, tombs and mausoleums. Neatly curbed cobblestone pathways lead to Section 6, where the headstone marking James Douglas Morrison can clearly been seen, despite a deluge of letters, drawings and posies. The site has a colourful history with Morrison courting controversy even after death. In 1981, Croatian sculptor Mladen Mikulin placed a bust of Morrison and a new gravestone at the site to commemorate the 10th anniversary of his death; but the bust was defaced through the years by cemetery vandals and later stolen in 1988. The current headstone bears an epitaph in Greek: '*Kata Ton Daimona Eaytoy*', which has been generally interpreted to mean 'True to his own spirit'. Spray-painted inscriptions have been added over time – the most obvious in crimson reads 'Light My Fire'. Marijuana is routinely left at the grave site and out-of-hours illegal visitations cause a nuisance. Needles, wine bottles and beer crates are testament to the parties that take place – but it isn't just litter that tests the patience of cemetery officials. Several attempts have been made to unearth Morrison's body – the act of fanatics, one assumes, or profiteers. Yet most rock music die-hards are content to relax under one of Père-Lachaise's large shady trees to soak up the serenity after paying quiet tribute to a unique voice and lyrical talent who remains, musically, immortal.

Contacts:
Cimetiere du Père-Lachaise
pere-lachaise.com

The Doors
thedoors.com

Paris Tourism
parisinfo.fr

MOSCOW, RUSSIA

Visitors who stand in the spot where Russian composer Pyotr Ilyich Tchaikovsky's final works were penned can be forgiven for feeling a little self-conscious. For anyone entering the composer's final home in the backwater of Klin are required to slip on a pair of o'er-the-shoes slippers, known as *bakhily*. Even the most elegant visitor will find it impossible not to shuffle. However, all that soft-shoe sliding on the property's ancient wooden floorboards keeps them polished to a high sheen. It also keeps the noise in the house to a minimum: it is near-silent, monastic even; which is exactly how Tchaikovsky liked it. Flick through the museum's own guide book, and you'll read that he yearned for 'a calm, quiet place for work'.

By the time he moved in to the property in 1892, Tchaikovsky used it as a refuge and sanctuary from the nuisance of international fame. He fled here to escape the critics, the press and his contemporaries. And it was here, in Klin, that he composed some of his greatest works. The town offered him anonymity, presented few distractions and suited his introverted character. Tchaikovsky craved privacy and left the high life of Moscow, 85 kilometres away, far behind without a care. Without the intrusive glare of the public eye he relished the purity of Mother Nature and the

Photo: Barichev

changing seasons. Before he sat down to write, he would wander through the simple villages and dark leafy forests to de-clutter his mind and allow the music to flow. Creative minds have always been inspired by nature and the sharp contrasts of winter, summer, spring and autumn. In Klin, Tchaikovsky enjoyed the spirit of the great outdoors – its birds, waterfowl, flowers, rain, trees, herbs, sunshine, fruits and nuts – with a childlike wide-eyed wonder. The bitter cold and freezing ice and snow of a Russian winter struck a chord with Tchaikovsky, who played around with the themes of hibernation, survival and the seasonal excitement of an awakening spring – a heart-warming analogy that has been used in fairy tales since the beginning of time.

The approach to the house is via a pretty path that riddles through handsome tree-scattered parklands. Though it is painted battleship grey, the property has both warmth and charm with its lace-like trellis decor around the verandas and in the gables. A neat garden is trimmed with the sort of blousy blooms and velvet-leafed shrubs that sent Tchaikovsky into raptures. Ferns, twiggy birds' nests, grasses, mossy boughs and tangled knots of tree roots – all have beauty. Tchaikovsky transformed the scenic splendour surrounding him into extraordinary melodies during the last year and a half of his life, from a table in his bedroom by a window overlooking the garden. Stand here, by this desk, and you are in the very spot where Tchaikovsky wrote his 'Symphony No. 6' – the piece into which he poured his 'whole soul', he stressed. Grand bookcases, portraits, objects d'art and family photographs rub shoulders with inky scores, age-stained correspondence and gifts from friends and admirers. Tchaikovsky was an intensely shy person who valued his close friendships. He suffered from anxiety that became more extreme the more he strove to keep his homosexuality secret. He was loyal and adoring with a strong admiration for Mozart – describing him as 'the musical Christ'. He was well-schooled, coming from a wealthy middle-class family, and was competent in French and German by the age of six. He also took piano lessons from an early age and sang in a choir.

Before pursuing a musical career in 1863, Tchaikovsky worked as a court clerk at the Ministry of Justice. He married a beautiful young woman named Antonina Miliukova, but the union was a disaster and the marriage was annulled within nine weeks (Tchaikovsky claimed it was because she lacked intelligence). After this, he entered into a relationship that was conducted purely by correspondence – perfect for a man with extreme shyness who was reluctant to consummate an affair. He developed a dependency on alcohol and after thirteen years of letters, the deeply sensitive Tchaikovsky was left devastated when his long-distance pen-and-paper relationship came to a halt unexpectedly and unexplained. His personal life remained turbulent – he is believed to have fallen in love with his own nephew – and Tchaikovsky constantly sought solace and comfort in music, ploughing considerable joy, pain, love and anguish into his compositions. Knowledge of his homosexuality, as well as its importance to his life and music, was suppressed in Russia by the Soviets, and has only recently become widely known in post-Soviet Russia. From his own diary entries over the years, it seems as if Tchaikovsky never reconciled himself with his sexuality and countered his bottled-up emotions, and life-long stage fright, with therapeutic bracing walks and periods of meditative isolation.

Tchaikovsky's brother Modest transformed the house into a museum in 1894 – a year after the composer's death. Though the cause of death has been subject to conspiracy theories, gossip and rumour, the most widely accepted explanation is that Tchaikovsky contracted cholera from unboiled drinking water. Since first throwing open its doors, the Tchaikovsky Museum has welcomed millions of visitors from all over the world, including a good many renowned composers and musicians who journey to Klin as a pilgrimage. Many pen notes of deep gratitude to the maestro that gave the world *Swan Lake* and *The Nutcracker*.

By train, the journey from Moscow's Leningradsky station to Klin is straightforward. A bus from Klin station (choose from numbers 5, 30, 37 or 40) passes the museum at 48 Tchaikovskogo Street. It's open 10am–6pm Friday to Tuesday (closed Wednesdays and Thursdays).

Contacts:
Tchaikovsky Museum
tchaikovsky-house-museum.ru

Alexander Tchaikovsky
tchaikovsky-research.org

Moscow Tourism
visitrussia.org.uk

STOCKHOLM, SWEDEN

It may have only opened a few short years ago, but ABBA: The Museum has stuck a big, fat pin on the world's great musical map. Stockholm is the proud host of the museum, which threw open its doors in May 2013. It excited the city, sent ABBA fans worldwide into a frenzy, and got an enthusiastic response from former band members too. So the city of Stockholm, Sweden and its four musical superstars joined forces. As you'd expect from Scandinavian design and Swedish ingenuity, the concept is delightfully unique.

ABBA's dark-bearded Björn Ulvaeus was particularly involved in ideas for the museum as he, coincidentally, lives close to the site. Given the museum's prominent spot in central Stockholm, Ulvaeus realised he would pass by it on foot dozens of times each year. It had to be good, he reasoned – very good. Otherwise he wouldn't be able to escape the embarrassment. And so it was that ABBA themselves became involved in this incredible all-singing, all-dancing tribute to Sweden's most famous musical export.

Housed within a building known as the Swedish Music Hall of Fame, the ABBA museum is the star of the show. It is a high-budget attraction with snazzy, beautifully crafted exhibits that range from a replica of the cottage on the island of Viggso where the group wrote many of their songs to a ritzy dressing room area filled with many of Abba's most famous sparkly tight-fitting costumes that fans can even try on. Have you dreamt of being in the band? Who hasn't! Whoever you want to be – either Björn, Benny, Anni-Frid or Agnetha – you can bop about on stage alongside your virtual ABBA band mates (glitter and all …). Not that visitors need to be absolute fanatics to enjoy the museum – there is so much insight, background and story that the exhibits are compelling even if you've never heard of the band. Everything revolves around the tale of four people accidentally meeting, falling in love and forming a group that went on to have great musical and lyrical success. The story is told through an audio guide produced by Catherine Johnson, who wrote the screenplay for the film *Mamma Mia!* She interviews each of the four members of ABBA separately and takes them on a trip down memory lane. It is moving; magical and soul-stirring. The whole thing feels interactive, as if ABBA are close by. There is nothing stuffy about this museum which mixes hi-tech gadgets with warmth and humour – to grand effect. Benny's studio is connected by a 'hot line' to a piano in the museum – when a red light flickers it means Benny is ready to tinkle the ivories and museum-goers are treated to a live rendition from afar. It is impossible not to pass the piano without crossing your fingers and whispering a prayer.

The seed was sown for ABBA: The Museum during the ABBAWORLD touring exhibition that visited Budapest, London, Prague, Melbourne and Sydney between 2009 and 2011. This gathered together band artefacts, concert footage, interviews and songs in historical context and started the whole interactive ball rolling. Today, the ticket that admits you contains an ID that generates a page on the museum website. Performing with the band, wearing glam ABBA gear and singing in the booth can be recorded by a simple scan of the ticket, so you can share the photos and videos on social media for 30 days after your visit.

You can't help but leave having understood 'ABBA: The Phenomenon' better and you'll have a special spring in your step, even if you're wearing platform-soled boots. TV footage of ABBA singing 'Waterloo' and winning the Eurovision Song Contest in Brighton in 1974 cannot help but get visitors dancing. Other exhibits provide some poignant memories around the break-ups and divorces in their personal lives.

ABBA formed in Stockholm in 1972 famously taking its name from the first letters of the member's names: Agnetha, Björn, Benny and Anni-Frid (better known as Frida). Björn and Benny wrote a song for the 1972 Eurovision Song Contest – 'Say It with a Song' – which was performed by Lena Anderson. It won third prize. A year later, ABBA themselves entered the 1973 Eurovision Song Contest with the song 'Ring Ring'. It also came third and debuted a new production technique, called the 'wall of sound' – the ABBA sound. In 1974, the group finally won the Eurovision Song Contest in Brighton, UK with 'Waterloo', which became ABBA's first UK number one and reached number six in the US charts. Their single 'SOS' became a UK top ten hit and in January 1976, 'Mamma Mia' made number one in the UK. Subsequent releases including 'Money, Money, Money', 'Knowing Me, Knowing You', and 'Dancing Queen' were all massive hits. In 1977, *ABBA: The Movie* – a feature film made of their Australian tour – became a huge cinematic success and signified ABBA the Mega-Group. Hits from this album were 'Take a Chance on Me', 'The Name of the Game', and 'Thank You for the Music'. The disco-inspired single 'Summer Night City' (1979) and album *Voulez-Vous* (1979) strengthened their popularity in the US. At the same time, 'Does Your Mother Know', 'Chiquitita', and 'I Have a Dream' all found their way into the charts. In January 1979, the group performed 'Chiquitita' at the Music for UNICEF Concert, donating all royalties for the song to the children's charity, in perpetuity. Their best-known disco hit 'Gimme! Gimme! Gimme! (A Man After Midnight)' was featured as a brand new track on the *Greatest Hits Vol. 2* (1979) album. The 1980s saw ABBA's style embrace deeply personal lyrics with the single 'The Winner Takes it All' in January 1980 spurring the biggest ever pre-order public demand for a UK album. Agnetha and Björn's marriage was unravelling and another hit single from this album was 'Lay Your Love on Me'.

The Visitors (1981) was their last studio album but didn't sell as well as other records. The last hit single 'One of Us' was a

Photo: Sharon Hahn Darlin

global hit in December 1981 as the world watched the band's marriages unravel and end in divorce. The band spent the summer of 1982 together, but nothing new was recorded and ABBA settled instead for a double compilation album of past hits, with two new songs thrown in. *The Singles: The First Ten Years* (1982) contained the new tracks 'Under Attack' and 'The Day Before You Came', which was the last song ABBA ever recorded together. At the end of 1983, ABBA disbanded to pursue their individual projects – though the popularity of the group didn't seem to wane at all with compilation albums achieving huge sales.

In April 2004, Björn, Benny and Frida travelled to London for the 30th anniversary of their Eurovision Song Contest win in 1974. They appeared on stage together after the fifth anniversary performance of *Mamma Mia!* the musical and in February 2005, all four former ABBA members appeared in public together, at the gala of *Mamma Mia!* in Stockholm – the first time since their disbandment in 1983. In October 2005, during the 50th anniversary of the Eurovision Song Contest held in Copenhagen, 'Waterloo' was voted best Eurovision song in the history of the contest. Even conservative estimates of ABBA's worldwide sales suggest the figure is around 400 million, making them the second most successful band of all time, after the Beatles. They are, without a doubt, the act that established Sweden in the mainstream music industry.

Buy tickets online, at SJ outlets near Stockholm's Central Station or when you arrive at the museum. While you're in the city there are plenty of opportunities to create your own ABBA walking tour around some of the other ABBA-related sights: Stockholm City Hall, where Benny Andersson first performed; The Royal Opera House, where Agnetha and Anni-Frid serenaded Queen Silvia and King Gustav with

'Dancing Queen' before the royal couple's wedding in 1976; and the handsome old town, where Anni-Frid and then-husband Benny Andersson once lived.

Contacts:
Abba Museum
abbathemuseum.com

ABBA
abbasite.com

Stockholm Tourism
visitstockholm.com

VIENNA, AUSTRIA

Vienna's musical heritage is unequalled by any other city in the world and of huge international renown. Inextricably linked to the waltz that bears its name, Austria's dazzling ballrooms pulsate with the rhythmic swirl of the Strauss masterpiece waltz *An der schönen blauen Donau* ('The Blue Danube'). For centuries, Vienna was the glittering seat of a great empire where the Habsburg dynasty and many of the aristocrats at the imperial court provided an excellent creative environment for musicians and artists. Many of the world's greatest composers were drawn to the city: imbibing the atmosphere and penning immortal works. Today, the Viennese musical tradition continues to attract legions of musical devotees keen to immerse themselves in the classics. The choice is immense: from Haydn and Beethoven to

Brahms, Schubert and Strauss with the irrepressible works of Wolfgang Amadeus Mozart enjoyed by millions all over the world.

For many, Joseph Haydn (1732–1809) is considered the doyen of Vienna's Classical era. He was sent to the city from his home on the edge of the Hungarian border at the age of eight, to join the famous St Stephen's Cathedral as a choirboy. Within a decade Haydn was composing his first classical works using the piano, organ and violin with great proficiency. After fulfilling the role of *kapellmeister* (musical director), overseeing two dozen musicians in the prestigious Esterházy Orchestra in Burgenland, he returned to Vienna to shine as the city's major classical star with Mozart one of his students. He spent some time in London, during 1791–92, and while there the University of Oxford awarded him an honorary doctorate of music. By 1795 the Esterházy Orchestra was resurrected by Prince Nikolaus II with Haydn at the helm once again. During this time he composed the string quartets 'Rider' and the 'Emperor Quartet' and the now world-famous song 'God Save the Emperor Franz' – a melody that eventually became the German national anthem and is still in use today. Mozart dedicated six string quartets to Haydn, his mentor, while Beethoven came all the way from Germany to take lessons from a man he called 'Papa' with great affection. At ease with life in Vienna, Haydn spent the last twelve years of his life in the limelight of the city, composing more than 100 symphonies, a great number of chamber music works, and numerous oratorios and masses.

Wolfgang Amadeus Mozart (1756–1791) followed in the footsteps of the much-admired Haydn to make Vienna his adopted home in 1781. As a child prodigy, Mozart had been tutored by his father and was presented to Europe as an accomplished performer at the age of five. Embarking on his first musical tour throughout Europe at that young age, he retained a home in the city of Vienna and remained fiercely loyal to its music scene until his death. He played for the Austrian royals at Schloss Schönbrunn and truly enchanted Empress Maria Theresa and the rest of the imperial family with his extraordinary talent. His enchanting compositions were received with great gusto by an adoring Vienna and when he fell in love with Constanze Weber, the proceeds from his successful opera *The Abduction from the Seraglio* (*Die Entführung aus dem Serail*) enabled him to get married to his sweetheart in the elegant St Stephen's Cathedral. Two years later, Mozart and his family moved to a spacious city apartment – the 'Mozarthaus' on Domgasse. The most productive period in his working life followed, during which time he composed piano concerti, chamber music works and the very famous opera 'The Marriage of Figaro' (*Die Hochzeit des Figaro*). Today, the Mozarthaus is a dedicated museum to all things Mozart-related and provides a fascinating narrative to his life in Vienna and its rich musical heritage. Mozart enjoyed the support of the city and its imperial court and thrived in a place with such great passion for the arts. He lived in Vienna until his death in 1791 with his last opera '*Die Zauberflöte*' ('The Magic Flute') premiering at the Theater auf der Wieden shortly before his untimely passing.

After receiving an early musical education from his father Johann, himself a professional musician, Ludwig van Beethoven moved from Germany to Vienna in 1787 as a child prodigy to work and study with Mozart and Haydn. Strongly bound to the city's aristocratic society, Beethoven first performed at the Vienna Burgtheater as a young boy in a concert dedicated to the monied elite who had given him such in-depth support. It was around the same time that his hearing impairment first became apparent: a condition

Photo: Schölla Schwarz

which was diagnosed as incurable in 1802. Despite rapid deterioration in his hearing, Beethoven composed the 'Eroica Symphony' and 'Symphony No. 5' during 1801 and 1808. In 1814 he presented his one and only opera, '*Fidelio*'. A year later, he conducted his last concert. With virtually no hearing, Beethoven composed 'Choral Symphony No. 9' and by 1818 he was profoundly deaf. By the time he died, he had moved house sixty-nine times during his thirty-five years in Vienna – many are marked with memorial plaques and two are considered of great note. The first is the apartment where he composed his Third Symphony, the 'Eroica,' and the second is where he wrote his 'Heiligenstädter Testament'.

Though Franz Schubert (1797–1828) was an ardent admirer of Beethoven, the pair never met. As a small, chubby child nicknamed *Schwammerl* (mushroom) by his peers, Schubert dedicated his entire childhood to musical pursuits, studying piano, organ, violin and developing his choral range. By the age of seventeen, he had already amassed a large body of works, including several piano pieces, string quartets, a three-act opera and his first symphony. Though his family persuaded him to take a teaching job his heart lay in music. He composed music for friends – later known as the *Schubertiads* – who were treated to songs like '*Der Wanderer*' and '*Die Forelle*'. At the age of 25, Schubert contracted syphilis and, unable to teach, fell into financial ruin. However, his output of heavenly compositions showed no sign of losing pace. He continued to create new work and by the time he died, aged 31, his portfolio amounted to almost 1,000 musical works, among them more than 600 lieder (solos), 9 symphonies (the eighth, 'The Unfinished', was deliberately never completed), numerous glorious chamber works and challenging piano music, some of which was never performed whilst he was alive. There has been a resurgence in musical evenings called Schubertiaden in Vienna – a modern tradition revived to honour Schubert's work.

Though he was born in Upper Austria, Anton Bruckner (1824–1896) lived and taught in Vienna for many decades. From an apartment wedged in a side alley by the Upper Belvedere Palace, Bruckner – a devout Christian – was known as 'God's Musician' for his spiritually uplifting symphonies, rich in heavenly melodies. It was an era that saw musical Vienna split into two factions: Bruckner's followers and the admirers of Johannes Brahms (1833–1897) – it was fashionable to be a die-hard follower of one or the other, never both. Hamburg-born Brahms chose Vienna as his home after he had toured through Europe performing his own music in concert. He was appointed manager of the Vienna Singers' Academy in 1862 and though he conducted at the Gesellschaft der Musikfreunde in Wien until 1875, Brahms secretly yearned for the life of a footless musician and envied the career of Johann Strauss Jnr. Like the rest of the musical world, Brahms bowed to the genius of Vienna's undisputed waltz king – the first son of Johann Strauss Snr, a famous musician himself. Though his father forbid him a musical career, Strauss Junior cared more for his violin than his schoolwork and would practice and practice for hours in secret to achieve perfection. The diligence paid off and in 1844 he performed his first concert to a standing ovation. His roaring success placed him in direction competition to his father and his flamboyant style triggered worldwide Strauss hysteria. Huge tours through Europe and America attracted sell-out crowds that propelled him to superstar status worldwide. Though he claimed the waltz crown the other members of the Strauss family also had considerable success composing waltzes and operettas – and not just his father. Brothers Josef (1827–1870) and Eduard (1835–1916) also contributed to the musical form that the world ultimately came to know as quintessentially Viennese.

Once deemed too risqué to be danced by couples other than those married to each other, the Viennese Waltz's sinful close holds earned it persecution for vulgarity. Originally a folk dance, the waltz was born out of peasant yodelling tunes and was eventually given a name derived from the German walzen meaning to roll, turn or glide. It finally gained some moral respectability following the French Revolution when attitudes loosened up on uptight dance floors Europe-wide. Today couples all over the world enjoy Vienna's spirited 180 beats-per-minute romps using time-worn dance steps to embark on a romantic voyage. Home-grown maestro Johann Strauss's 'The Blue Danube' was given a new lease of life when it featured on *The Blue Danube: 2001 Space Odyssey* in 1968, giving the waltz a resurgence in popularity. Forty years on, Vienna's jovial whirling jaunt continues to captivate couples keen to master its charm and mystique.

Unlike the sluggish pace of its more sedate English cousin, the Viennese Waltz is a fast-tempo rotary dance packed with change steps and turns that require light, nimble feet. Frequent clockwise (natural) or anti-clockwise (reverse) footwork demands plenty of agility while good stamina is essential to maintain floor-work at a rapid rate. Yet with excellent tips and tuition, almost any Cinderella and Prince can go to the ball, according to the city's waltzing kings. And nobody in Vienna wants to be caught, come November's celebrated ball season, unable to move with finesse.

Austria's capital hosts hundreds of balls during a dazzling three-month season, when more than 300 events issue gilded invitations city-wide. At this time, Vienna's Musikvereinssaal concert hall transforms itself into a swish chandelier-bedecked ballroom for the oh-so prestigious Philharmonic Ball. Hosted by an organisation, guild or institution, each ritzy event attracts VIP guests of luminaries from the world of arts and film – each with a shared adoration for Vienna's super-charged waltz.

Austria's capital provides music buffs with a bewildering choice of pilgrimages along Beethoven, Haydn, Strauss and Schubert themes. Organised tours lead visitors around the sites linked with Vienna's most famous characters of classical music. Bold, baroque and achingly beautiful: the history-rich, storied streets offer a fascinating stroll through its musical tradition back to the time of the formidable Austro-Hungarian Empire. Paths wind their way past Vienna's striking monumental architecture, dazzling palaces, grand mansions and opulent facades. Epitomising decadence in all its glory, the vast Hofburg Palace – the imposing royal home of the Habsburg family for over six centuries with its lavish gilded decor and fascinating heritage – and the famous nearby gothic spires of St Stephen's Cathedral have both welcomed composers of enviable repute. Stone backstreets lend a magical mystery to pedestrians seeking out the angelic soul-stirring chorus of the Vienna Boys' Choir – a simple, pure sound that contrasts perfectly with the ostentatious pomp of Vienna's State Opera House (*Staatsoper*), home to the world-renowned Vienna Philharmonic Orchestra.

Contacts:
Vienna Tourist Board
wien.info

Waltz Balls
waltzballs.org

Austria Tourism
austria.info

GHENT, BELGIUM

Though it is undoubtedly overshadowed by the more famous cities of Brussels and Bruges, Belgium's third city of Ghent has a unique spirit and character that ensures it shouldn't be overlooked. Quirky, eccentric and gutsy, Ghent mixes a funky arts scene with a strong musical heritage. *Gentenaars* embrace everything that indulges the senses, from some of Europe's most famous street-art to a heartfelt passion for music with a transatlantic link. For as well as the bold sweeping brush strokes of the city's vibrant murals, galleries, studios and artists, Ghent is also the home of the Belgian underground rock scene with its record labels, basement bars and venues. Yep, the city makes a lot of noise – in all of its artistic genres: psychedelic hip-hop, curbside sculpture, sludge grunge, graffiti art, rock DJs, installations and experimental crazy jazz.

One reason why so much good music emerges from Ghent is that every would-be artist has plenty of opportunity to hone their craft. Innumerable studios, practice rooms and local gigs offer bands the space to cut their teeth. Free concerts sweep through the city almost every week with music filling the streets throughout the summer. In every newspaper and corner shop window you'll see advertisements for guitar lessons, voice coaches and band auditions. Few cities in the world the size of Ghent boast so many stages. At the heart of this exciting cultural centre is the Vooruit Arts Centre: a legendary venue that prides itself on crossover acts that combine visual arts and music. What's more, Ghent Jazz Festival more than quadruples the music offering in the city when a host of local and international jazz bands, solo artists and unofficial buskers and street bands rock up each July (see: gentjazz.com). Ghent becomes a music-lover's Mecca as it welcomes hundreds of performers and thousands of fans.

Ghent has pedigree in the musical realm – two graduate schools teach opera and musicianship. Pop-up venues add to the city's remarkable musical character and the enigmatic variety of performances. During the OdeGand celebrations in mid-to-late September, a single ticket grants you access to more than 60 concerts centred along Ghent's elegant avenues and reed-trimmed canals – an impressive location for some truly creative world rock music. In late August to early September, the whole city becomes a series of concert stages for every genre of Ghent's home-spun music. Jazz in 't Park is free and centred around the city's greens spaces. Showcasing Belgian contemporary jazz in all its many guises, from light easy-listening to freeform, the event features established names and upcoming local talent and is a proud supporter of new artists. Visual art enhances every musical showcase in an overflowing fusion of animation, art, sound and spectacle.

So what of the transatlantic connection?

Ghent has a lasting North American link born out of the role it played over 200 years ago as the city in which England and the United States signed the Treaty of Ghent. Negotiated in the city, and adopted on Christmas Eve 1814, the treaty formally ended the War of 1812 between England and the United States in the North American phase of the Napoleonic Wars. Today, you may find that some of Ghent's thin scattering of tourists have a North American vibe. Some bring their guitars with them; others a saxophone. Many head to the Club de Gand on Groentenmarkt – a backstreet acoustic music venue that welcomes jazz,

Photo: Wernervc

flamenco, gypsy folk, classical, blues and much, much more. Keen to soak up the scene and meet the movers and shakers? Then head to the Kinky Star Club in Vlasmarkt to hang out with a mix of Ghent's musicians, DJs and assorted artists – this popular hotspot hosts two concerts each week, from unsigned bands and jamming sessions to famous faces. Another musical joint not to be missed can be found on Nieuwevaart – the lively Café de Loge is a moodily-lit venue for concerts, theatre, comedy and other arty nights and is accessed through an old garage door. The Charlatan has a more mainstream party vibe with a trio of different dance floors, the best DJs in town and weekly free concerts. Yet with a brave love of every genre of music, this bass-crazy place on Vlasmarkt is anything but dull. Elsewhere in Ghent, visitors can expect to find all sorts of musical pursuits from guitar solo marathons, singing contests and battles of the bands to blues nights, classical cruises and hell-raising rock operas.

Contacts:
Ghent Jazz Festival
ghentjazz.com

Ghent Festival
gentfestival.be

Ghent Tourism
visit.gent.be/

BERLIN, GERMANY

Since the Fall of the Wall, Berlin has undergone a phenomenal transformation from a land divided by Cold War politics and a 100-mile barrier of concrete, electrified fences, watchtowers and razor-wire to a vibrant, open city of 3.5 million residents that shout loud and proud about its musical legacy. Nestled in North-western Germany on the banks of Rivers Spree and Havel, Berlin has entered a bright, new chapter of its history that now incorporates musical influences from all corners of the globe. When the Wall crumbled in 1989, Berlin's artists, musicians and creative intellectuals – from East and West – congregated in a single neighbourhood as part of the glue of reunification. Today, in Mitte the native Berliners and other nationalities who have settled there are dazzling the rest of Europe with their bold creativity and quietly self-assured zeal.

Everything musical in Berlin has appeared to treble in amplified energy since 1989. It has always had a hip, cool and kooky character but now it is more confident and even more eclectic, with modern Berlin a byword for trailblazing the cutting-edge. As one of the great cities of the world celebrated for their artsy culture, Berlin's music has always been ambitious. Many of the world's most respected musicians have claimed this most inspiring of cities as their own personal soundtrack, including David Bowie, Nick Cave, Lou Reed and Iggy Pop. Every techno DJ in the world has been shaped by Berlin's pumping techno scene, which pioneered an entire electronic generation. After living in the city for three years during the mid-to-late 1970s, David Bowie – who recorded three albums there whilst sharing a flat with Iggy Pop – did much to bring the musical joys of

Berlin to his loyal devotees during the crazy highs of his career. His time in the city, learning from the unknown knob-twiddling phaser-pushing techno maestros, together with the madcap parties he enjoyed, have passed into hedonistic rock folklore. Though the decades have passed, the adventurous spirit that drew Bowie to Berlin remains alive and kicking at every turn. Musical pilgrims can join one of the trips around all the old Bowie hangouts on a Fritz Music Tour (priced from 15 euros per person) – worth it for the salacious titbits and lesser-known backstage secrets alone. You'll start at the famous Hansa Studios right in the heart of Berlin, directly on Potsdamer Platz, which was once an office building, built in 1912. As the place where much of Berlin's iconic music was created, Hansa Studios has welcomed countless superstar artists through its doors – not just David Bowie but also U2, R.E.M., Peter Maffay, Nina Hagen and Udo Jürgens. Since it opened in the 1960s, the Hansa Studio has undergone a reduction in the number of its studios but what remains is flooded with daylight, equipped with classic analogue and digital equipment, and boasts exceptional acoustics. Something spine-tingling happens when you enter Studio 1 and all the hairs on the back of your neck stand on end – I suspect the reason is sheer nostalgic buzz from a singular history of a bygone musical era. Berlin also has the Tonstudio 2 where Bowie recorded 'Low' and 'Heroes', and produced *The Idiot* for Iggy Pop, and where British bands like Depeche Mode, Supergrass and Snow Patrol have since laid down tracks.

On a Fritz Music Tour, the commentary comes at a mile a minute, while the van stereo pumps out favourite David Bowie, Iggy Pop and U2 tracks along the way. Screeching around the city to loud music lends a special vibe to exploring Berlin's musical character. First Tonstudio, then the apartment building on Hauptstrasse where Bowie and Pop planned their collaborations in between all manner of rock star shenanigans with a party crowd of artists, activists and pleasure-seekers. In the same street you'll find a legendary gay bar where the pair used to hang out and where a portrait of Bowie remains.

Next it is the Hotel Ellington, a former Nazi guest house that also boasts a colourful musical heritage that can give any hotel in LA a run for its money. During 1949, when the surrounding area was occupied by US troops, the cellar played host to the Badewanne club in which Duke Ellington, Dizzy Gillespie and Ella Fitzgerald used to play. In the 70s, it reopened as pumping techno bar Dschungel with a regular clientele that included Bowie, Iggy Pop, Lou Reed and, later, Nick Cave. It closed and lay vacant for a while in 1993 but is now experiencing a renaissance as one of Berlin's hippest art deco hotels. Black and white photos of Gillespie, Ellington and Fitzgerald adorn the walls and regular jazz concerts take place in the bar and attract a mixed crowd of jazz diehards. Other blasts from the past with an Iggy and Bowie connection include legendary punk venue S036, which continues to champion unsigned new wave bands.

In amongst the street art and bright daubs of graffiti, you'll find a heady mix of punk clothing, political poster stores, DJ bars and record shops selling anything from techno to bluegrass and indie. For a true vinyl splurge, head to Rock Steady Records to trawl through a five-star archive of over 10,000 LPs – including plenty from Bowie's heyday, stacks of vintage Kraftwerk and virtually every synthesiser band that followed in the German group's wake. Though they hailed from Dusseldorf, Kraftwerk (the name means power-plant) inspired the flood of new techno, ambient, and experimental electronic sounds of the '90s. Berlin embraced Kraftwerk's catalogue and the robotic, conceptual ideas it experimented with, integrating mechanised sounds from everyday life into music. In surrounding galleries you'll see plenty of funky collaborations between designers, photographers, media types, performance artists and creatives keen to transcend the forty-year partition of Germany in bold, brave areas of work. Almost 200 museums, innumerable historic monuments, riverside promenades, lakeside cafés, beer gardens and fine restaurants wow first-time visitors. When it marked the 25th anniversary of reunification, Berlin simply promised to continue its urban and social reinvention in a bid to cement its place as one of world's most fast-paced, forward-thinking cities. Now that is refreshing.

Bowie's time in Berlin wasn't contained to a single decade; he revisited often, playing a three-day open-air concert in the divided city in 1987: a performance that many still view as having helped change history. Standing in front of the Reichstag, Bowie chose 'Heroes' for his performance and not even the Wall could keep the song from the East. The concert made it onto the airwaves and was held near enough to the border that many East Berliners crowded along the wall to listen to the forbidden music wafting across from the West. Bowie spoke to the crowd, in German: 'We send our wishes to all our friends who are on the other side of the wall.' 'Heroes' is haunted by the Cold War themes of fear and isolation that hung over the city at the time, where two lovers from either side of the divide hopelessly attempt to find a way to be together.

The British rock band Genesis also performed at the three-day show and it was during their act that the East German police cracked down on young East Berliners. Using water cannons to attack the crowds, the police then arrested more than 200 people, dragging them away forcibly in unmarked blacked-out vans.

Another trip saw Bowie in a nostalgic mood, with Berlin playing a central role in the 2013 release of his first song in 10 years. 'Where Are We Now?' was released on his birthday, and the accompanying video featured Bowie strolling the streets of his much-loved Berlin. He seeks out places from his past, including an auto repair shop downstairs from his old apartment as he sings, 'Had to get the train, from Potsdamer Platz ...'

On a practical note, tourists are well-served by the city's 770 hotels, 50 airlines and excellent links via rail, bus and road. Away from the buzz of Berlin's music hubs, there are plenty of other compelling sightseeing attractions, from bullet-scarred WWII attractions, golf, luxury spas, cabaret acts, 900 bars and 200 clubs to river cruises, cycle tours, designer shopping, wine tasting or dining at 4,700 eateries. And there are, of course, also the remnants of The Wall.

Contacts:
Berlin Tourism
visitberlin.de

David Bowie
davidbowie.com

German Tourism
germany.travel

REYKJAVIK, ICELAND

When Icelandic singer Björk was a little girl, she loved nothing more than exploring the frozen tundra of her homeland, and would stroll across the stark, ragged terrain singing at the top of her lungs. Iceland – the Land of Fire and Ice – is so much more than Björk's native home, it is her inspiration: a brooding, bubbling and beautiful volcanic terrain of hissing geothermal geysers cloaked in wisps of sulphuric mist. The otherworldly Icelandic landscape has a hypnotic quality: chilling, fizzing and spitting, with rich flashes of red and dark, inky hues. Björk feels a kinship with the Icelandic landscape's feral wonder and you can hear this passion in the power of her haunting vocal style. Her music captures the moody isolation, epic skies and moss-scattered craters of her homeland. The music and Iceland are both extraordinarily beautiful: wave-carved and wind-swept by Mother Nature, to whom Björk feels spiritually tethered. It seems bold, big, mighty, intense and unafraid yet mystical and curious: fairytale awe packed with a climactic punch. Nothing prepares you for the magnificent sight of pink clouds shifting over fields of charcoal-grey and brilliant yellow gorse dappled by slanted purple shadows.

For many fans, Björk was the first time they had heard music from Iceland and her distinctive sound quickly established her among the most unique artists of our time. She burst onto the European music scene as the lead singer of alternative band The Sugarcubes: then known by her full name Björk Guðmundsdóttir. As a prolific song-writer, Björk sang and played music from an early age, releasing her first album when she was only twelve. Her unique kookiness attracted plenty of attention from Icelandic record labels and before joining The Sugarcubes she was in a number of bands, including Spit and Snot, Jam-80 and Exodus. Today, as a global star she has undoubtedly helped pave the way for Icelandic artists to aim far more than a local audience. The 20-strong, all-female hip-hop outfit Reykjavíkurdætur, the quirky garage-punk of Grísalappalísa and electronica of GusGus have all benefited from Björk's legacy. All have cited the Icelandic landscape as playing an important role in the evolution of their craft. Lyrics describe the freedom of the space, the peace that comes from solitude and the living, breathing, shifting character of Iceland and its tectonic plates.

Outlandish dresses, kaleidoscopic hair, bizarre ghost-like make-up and an impish face. Exaggerated geometric designs, jewellery like puffed popcorn, headdresses created from metallic swirls and an angelic voice that trills like a tinkling wind-chime. Eyes that stare into the camera, occasionally half-closing to shoot the audience a quizzing, conspiratorial look. Björk is half-person, half-leprechaun, with a spellbinding allure, as if she sprinkles everything around her with glitter dust. She is an activist too, campaigning for the preservation of some of Iceland's bleakest stretches that come under threat, from time to time, in the pursuit of oil and gas. An environmentalist of some conviction, Björk is at her virtuosic best when she is going bonkers in a song about a bird, a tree or a mollusc or whispering about the eerie calm of a lagoon. She had a bohemian upbringing, growing up with her parents in a hippy commune and listening to Jimi Hendrix. Even as a very young girl, she can remember being totally invigorated by the natural environment, opting to spend days alone in a tent watching the sky, climbing rocks and studying the wind. Little did she know then that she would

Photo: A.Maldon

one day work with the great Sir David Attenborough on a film of her live show, *Biophilia*. Attenborough, who is a huge fan of the project, has narrated the film, which consists of '10 songs with 10 emotions and 10 connections to the natural world'. Iceland is the perfect setting for such a concept, as a biophiliac's paradise with its plunging waterfalls, twisting lava extrusions and gin-clear, sparkling, glacial lakes. Indeed Iceland is so endowed with theatrical natural wonders, with its primordial scree, thunderous waterfalls, silica-laden textured landforms, steam plumes and fiery volcanoes, that it has been used as the film set for *Game of Thrones*. That it has the Aurora Borealis, or 'Northern Lights', too is the icing on the cake for a wilderness nation too blessed. Like Björk's lyrics, Iceland boasts characteristics that are dizzily surreal with cut-glass ice-caps that emit eerie moans and huge expanses of penetrating silence. There are luminous icy-blue depths, dreamy weightlessness and shafts of yellow sun that dance above blood-red pools. Little wonder that Iceland has successfully stirred the creative juices of writers, playwrights, painters, sculptors and photographers over the centuries and inspired musicians, such as Echo & the Bunnymen, to feature this magical land on the cover of their albums. Listen to arguably Björk's best album, *Homogenic*, and you'll be transported to the Land of Fire and Ice in all its geothermal splendour with its plums, rhyolite mountains and lunar-like basalt formations and stunning northern-most reaches.

Contact:
Iceland Tourism
visiticeland.com

Björk
bjork.com

Island Landscape Tours
icelandtours.is

VENICE, ITALY

Though his name is known around the world for his highly-accessible composition 'The Four Seasons', not much is understood about Antonio Vivaldi away from his craft. This can prove a source of frustration to anyone seeking to trace the career one of history's greatest violinists. For though he was born, lived and worked in Venice for most of his life, very little remains to tell history much about Vivaldi the man. What we can gather, however, is that the violin virtuoso had a tumultuous existence: enjoying a rich and privileged life but dying in abject poverty.

On 4 March 1678 Antonio Vivaldi was born in the city of Venice to a musical family. In May 1678, little Antonio was baptised in the beautiful Gothic church of San Giovanni in Bragora, the parish of his family – today there is a plaque next to the baptismal font. Though there is no record of the family home, we know that his violinist father – Giovanni Battista Vivaldi – was a much-respected teacher at St Mark's Basilica. With a mop of red hair, Vivaldi grew up in and around the great Venetian churches, his tiny footsteps echoing through the cloisters.

As an older boy, he embarked on an ecclesiastical career, studying theology in the church of San Geminianus, then situated in front of St Mark's Basilica. He earned the nickname *il prete rosso* ('the reddish priest') on account of his ginger hair.

After being ordained in 1703, Vivaldi chose music over the priesthood. His active career was devoted to teaching at the Pietà Church before accepting the conductor role at the same institution. Under Vivaldi's direction, this orchestra flourished and achieved an international reputation. Vivaldi remained at the Pietà for over 30 years, whilst simultaneously working as a manager at the glittering Sant'Angelo Theatre. It is here, amongst an ever-changing sea of creative influences, that he wrote the most memorable of his works.

Vivaldi's output was a mix of vocal and instrumental music, both sacred and secular. He was extremely productive, composing over 700 pieces during his lifetime, ranging from sonatas to concertos to operas. Though Vivaldi's vocal music is little known today, he was acclaimed for his operas in his day and these were in great demand in Venice and further afield throughout Italy. Yet it is his exquisite mastery of the violin that is best remembered 300 years later, and the extraordinary demands he placed on technique in order to reach new heights. Most of his sonatas were written for one or two violins and of his concertos, 221 are for solo violin and orchestra. Most of these are formed of a trio of movements, arranged in the order of fast, slow, fast. Within the movements, the music is designed as solo passages that alternate with passages for the full orchestra. Layering the sounds like this, between a soloist and an orchestra, adds greater theatre as it allows tempo and tension to slowly build. It was a technique that Johann Sebastian Bach (1685–1750) greatly admired, and would later emulate. Indeed, throughout Europe's musical circles in the 18th century, Vivaldi was held in high regard.

Vivaldi travelled a great deal to take his compositions to the musical audiences in Vienna, the Netherlands and a host of cities across Italy. For reasons that aren't exactly clear, Vivaldi left Venice for the final time in 1740. However, on this occasion he was never to return. Vivaldi died a poor and forgotten man in a small house in central Vienna, where the famous Hotel Sacher stands today, right behind the Vienna Opera House. His body was laid to rest in a mass grave where the Vienna Technical University in Karlsplatz is today. There is no tombstone.

As a visitor in Venice today, there are innumerable modern-day mementoes of Vivaldi, such as souvenirs depicting the virtuosi with violin tucked under his chin; bars that have cocktails named in his honour (*La Primavera* – 'Spring') and posters advertising performances of his music. For a chance to fill in some of the blanks and search to resolve some of the unanswered questions that relate to the change in fortunes of Vivaldi's life, it may help to pay a visit to the Vivaldi Museum. It isn't a mammoth collection, but this small, private exhibit is interesting nonetheless. There are plenty of documents, artefacts and manuscripts to pore over and some instruments with which Vivaldi taught the girls at the Pietà Church Orphanage music. The curator has some fascinating stories to share, but the general public need to prearrange a visit by appointment. However this ensures the experience is intimate and gloriously un-rushed. Tel: 041 5222171, email: cultura@pietavenezia.org.

Numerous concerts of Vivaldi's music take place in Venice throughout the year, with 'The Four Seasons' the most popular show. Venues include the Pietà Church, pietavenezia. org with other super events celebrating Vivaldi's works organised by Interpretative Venice interpretiveneziani.com. Virtuosi Di Venezia is a Trip Advisor winner for its excellent calendar of classical shows, including year-round Vivaldi offerings, see: virtuosidivenezia.com.

For Vivaldi pilgrims this is probably the most rewarding way to pay homage to one of the greatest violinists of all time, for in the absence of an obvious landmark of his life in his city, the Baroque musical legacy of Vivaldi is left to speak for itself. And it is bliss.

Ever since he was a child, Vivaldi loved nature and had watched in wide-eyed awe at the way the outside world awakened and unfolded. In 'The Four Seasons', he created beautiful and expressive scenes of spring, summer, autumn and winter. For spring, the passage commences after the long winter in which the landscape is covered in thick snow. Then, spring arises like a colourful explosion with the flowers, the butterflies and the song of the birds bursting to life. It is a joyous passage, with added warbles and trills and the gentle babble of a little stream, before a heavy shower and a clap of thunder and a bolt of lightning. This first movement depicts a tranquil scene of a place where a shepherd soundly sleeps, in a gentle murmuring breeze. A sweet violin solo describes the beautiful dream of the little shepherd. The third movement is jubilant, heralding spring.

In summer, Vivaldi creates a slow, steady heat that musically describes the rhythmic sultriness of warm nights and the languid song of the lark at sunset. In this second movement a farmer returns home after a tiring day on the land but is unable to sleep due to thunderclaps that interrupt his slumber. The powerful forces of nature are unleashed as a storm ensues.

Autumn is a joyous celebration of the harvest, a happy time when crops are gathered and fruits picked. Then, suddenly and abruptly, the celebratory tone stops. A single quiet melody denotes a nap after too much food and drink. It is calm, and the sound of crisp autumnal leaves being caught by a brisk wind is like a flurry of crunching confetti.

This third movement starts with hunting, a favourite sport during Vivaldi's era. It is a playful melody with an imitated sound of a hunting horn before the search, chase and cull of the prey.

The first notes of winter echo the slow fall of snowflakes with chattering teeth in the cold, depicted by the fast trill of violins. A gust of wind shakes the snow as the tempo increases. Rain is the theme of this fourth movement and the scene is safe and warm as raindrops begin to rhythmically fall. A violin solo describes the cosiness of home. In this movement, the orchestra imitates a smooth burst of wind that grows in intensity to reach storm strength. This is the end of the piece, a great creation: and the atmospheric cycle the nature's four seasons.

Contacts:
Music in Venice
musicinvenice.com

Italian Tourism
italia.it

WARSAW, POLAND

When Frederic Chopin was born in 1810, Warsaw was a gritty sprawl of industrial urbanisation with a history that boasted more twists and turns than a Graham Greene thriller. A steely determination has served Warsaw's residents well as, time after time, their city rises from the ashes. Buildings have been ruined, castles reduced to rubble, palaces ransacked and plundered and entire neighbourhoods razed to the ground. Its biggest challenge by far was its near-total destruction during the Second World War: a painstaking rebirth that re-created Warsaw's Old Town in meticulous detail, earning it coveted UNESCO World Heritage Site status for its efforts. Today the city is testimony to a remarkable heroism, commitment and national pride, that wasn't evident in its early history. Warsaw was established relatively late in Polish history, beginning life as a small string of fishing huts. For several centuries, it was way down the list of Poland's most important cities – until, that is, the union of Poland and Lithuania in 1596, when centrally-positioned Warsaw found itself the nation's new capital. It recovered from a brutal Swedish invasion (1655–1660) and achieved a steady rise to prosperity during the 18th century when the rest of Poland was undergoing devastating economic decline. Cultural and artistic life flourished at around the time Frederic Chopin came into the world and went on to thrill his homeland with his music.

Chopin was born to a French father, Nicolas Chopin, and a Polish mother, Tekla Justyna Krzy anowska. As a young boy, he showed early enthusiasm for piano music and had composed two polonaises by the time he reached seven. Chopin impressed Polish audiences in those early years with accomplished concert performances. His parents ensured he received a good education and arranged for him to study music privately with Joseph Elsner, founder and director of the Warsaw Conservatory. At sixteen, Chopin became a full-time piano student under Elsner and excelled in theory, harmony and melody and became fascinated by *Mazovian* folk melodies. He famously played his last performance in Warsaw in October 1830, before moving to Paris permanently. Chopin based his life and work in the French capital until his death at 39 years of age in 1849.

Today Warsaw is justifiably proud of its world-famous pianist and welcomes legions of classical music fans to its magnificent palatial venues for dazzling concerts. A fine array of elegant venues delight in staging Chopin's mazurkas and polonaises, performed by well-known Polish pianists. Tour companies also run a number of guided city sightseeing tours that following in Chopin's footsteps around Warsaw's storied Old Town.

Enjoy a scenic walk the along the Royal Route to reach the apartment where Chopin lived before he moved to Paris. Owned by the Chopin Museum, Chopin's former home is equipped with some of the maestro's personal effects together with fine furniture from the era, including a piano owned by the famous pianist and composer Franz Liszt, glass and porcelain pieces, and portraits of Chopin's parents and cousins. This beautiful building also contains some rare antique etchings of Warsaw from the early 19th century as well as some of Chopin's scribbled notes and draft manuscripts.

From there, head to the Holy Cross Church on Krakowskie Przedmiescie where Chopin's heart is stored in a funerary casket. When Chopin died his body was buried in Paris but his heart was taken to Warsaw, as per his deathbed request. It was preserved in what is believed to have been a jar of cognac and smuggled into the Polish city before being interred in a pillar at the Holy Cross Church. However, in 2014 in a secret midnight exhumation, the heart was removed for urgent inspection. A team of thirteen experts, including scientists, officials and the Archbishop of Warsaw were present and sworn to secrecy. Hundreds of photographs were taken, the composer's heart was checked thoroughly and a new, thicker, hot wax seal was added to the jar to prevent further evaporation of the original amber-coloured

Photo: Adrian Grycuk

Photo: Adrian Grycuk

preservative liquid. Before it was returned to its resting place in the church's pillar, the Archbishop said prayers over the heart – the next scheduled check of the 170-year-old organ isn't due now until 2064. A biblical passage inscribed on the pillar reads: 'For where your treasure is, there your heart will be also.' Chopin's elder sister Ludwika co-ordinated the shipment of the heart from Paris, where the rest of his remains lie in the Père-Lachaise Cemetery.

Though Chopin is widely believed to have contracted tuberculosis, mystery surrounds how he managed to survive for so long with such a chronic medical condition, casting doubt on this assumption. Scientists have also questioned how it was possible that he continued to pen pieces of such extraordinary beauty while he was close to death. The Chopin Society in London suggests that Chopin bore the symptoms of cystic fibrosis, a claim that is backed up by a leading Polish cystic fibrosis specialist. Certainly Chopin was weak from early childhood and prone to chest infections, wheezing and coughing. Cystic fibrosis is a genetic illness which clogs the lungs with excess thick and sticky mucus. Chopin was chronically underweight, another tell-tale symptom of cystic fibrosis. Few cystic fibrosis sufferers live past 40 and Chopin's untimely death occurred when he was 39. Pre-2014, the last time Chopin's heart was checked in the hermetically-sealed jar was just after the end of the Second World War, according to Poland's National Fryderyk Chopin Institute.

Nineteenth-century German composer Robert Schumann described Chopin's music as 'cannons hidden among flowers' meaning that Chopin's music was, and remains, a symbol of Poland's long struggle for freedom. Nazi Germany banned it for that very reason. Yet it was a German general, Erich von dem Bach, who saved the stored heart from oblivion amid the relentless Nazi bombing of occupied Warsaw in 1944.

The Polish government like to say that Chopin died from homesickness and there is truth to this suggestion as the composer was utterly heartbroken at leaving his homeland behind. A commemorative poem by Norwid, entitled 'Chopin's Piano', describes him fondly as: 'Varsavian by birth, Pole by heart, global citizen by talent'.

Another must-see Chopin landmark in the city is the exhibit at the Frederic Chopin Museum, a fastidiously-gathered collection of artefacts, documents and compositions located in the grandiose setting of the Baroque-era Ostrogowskich Castle. Mixing historical exhibitions with high-tech multi-media, this biographical museum draws on all aspects of Chopin's life, from birth to death. This is a well-conceived homage to the greatest Polish composer, providing an in-depth insight to the man, his passion and his creative success.

Don't miss a chance to snap a photo at the Royal Park in Lazienki, where the famous monument dedicated to the composer proudly stands. This is, without doubt, the most beautiful park in Warsaw – and the statue is fittingly handsome: a fine bronze of the artist sitting under a willow tree. The original, created in 1926, was destroyed during the war in 1940. It was rebuilt in 1958 and today it is a popular place for music recitals and concerts. For evening concerts of Chopin's favourite pieces, take a look at the annual calendar of performances at Warsaw's National Philharmonic Hall.

For traditional Polish soul food, visit the Restaurant Honoratka on Winnicka, an old family-run Warsaw eatery often frequented by Chopin who dined well on hearty soups, pickled vegetables and roast game with dumplings.

In the small town of Zelazowa Wola, around 50 kilometres west of Warsaw, you'll find the birthplace of Frederic Chopin. Though he only spent the first seven months of his life in the small manor house, the home is conserved as a museum.

Phases of Chopin's life are set on a timeline accompanied by a variety of personal belongings, documents, manuscripts, paintings and sculptures. Close by in Brochow you'll find the 16th-century Parish church where his parents were married (in 1806) and the composer himself baptised. An inscription on the font reads: 'Baptized in this church on 23 April 1810 was Fryderyk Chopin, born on 22 February 1810 at Zelazowa Wola.'

Soak up the charm of Castle's Square where between 1826–1831 a building stood belonging to the Sisters Bernadine with a music school lead by Joseph Elsner, Chopin's music teacher. On Krakowskie Przedmiescie look out for the Res Sacra Miser building: it was here that young Chopin gave his first public concerts, at Namiestnikowski Palace and the Church of the Nuns of the Visitation. Chopin's family (by now Frederic was one of four children) moved into Kazimierz Palace here in 1817 and lived in Krakowskie Przedmiescie for ten years. It was here that his parents established a guesthouse for boys and created a fine Botanic Garden.

Chopin lived in the grounds of the opulent Saxon Palace on Saxon Square for a few years of his life, moving here in 1810 and occupying the right wing when his father became a music teacher in the high school. Be sure to allow enough time to stroll through the leafy gardens of Saxon Park, where the musician and his sister played chase and hide-and-seek – the views are breathtaking. Memories of his time there helped inspire Chopin to produce some of his earliest Romantic pieces and arguably the finest body of solo music for the piano. Preludes, nocturnes, waltzes: Chopin composed some of the greatest, but he claimed they weren't complex: 'Simplicity is the final achievement. After one has played a vast quantity of notes and more notes, it is simplicity that emerges as the crowning reward of art.'

Contacts:
Ula Chopin Tours
ulawarsawtours.com

Visit Warsaw
warsaw.com

Warsaw City Tours
warsawcitytours.info

KAUSTINEN FOLK FESTIVAL, FINLAND

In Finland, the phenomena known as the 'midnight sun' has inspired artists and songwriters for centuries. Instead of nightfall, the sun merely dips down towards the sea, rising almost instantly – red and refreshed – as if it had been down to drink. During the summer months, Finland is almost constantly illuminated by sunshine, often with very little discernible difference between day and night. While the earth is rotating at a tilted axis relative to the sun, the sun never sets above the Arctic Circle and so Finns spend long, lazy days soaking up warm rays, and relishing the joys of the summertime after the harsh, bitter cold of the winter months. Congregating around sparkling fish-filled lakes and flower-filled meadows with friends and family they celebrate the summer landscape as an egg-yolk amber sun sends a warm glow across the horizon, amidst a slowly-unfolding sky of crimson-pink hues.

Folk music in Finland has had something of a revival over the last few years. Between Bob Dylan nostalgia and the emergence of exciting home-grown acts, it has managed

to shed its stale image. Today, Finns enjoy both the classic tunes that have long been identified as part of their national identity as well as new, young, acoustic musicians. Finnish folk combines the musical traditions of past, present and future, incorporating a broad mix of balladeers, fiddlers and strummers. Some has its origins in the poetic *runo*-song, a harmony-rich genre found in the other Nordic countries, as well parts of Estonia and Russia, with other styles beginning as an oral story-telling tradition, adding instruments and timbres over time.

One of the catalysts for Finland's epic folk revival is the Kaustinen Folk Music Festival, which takes place in the country's mid-northwest. Since it was established in 1968, it has rapidly become the biggest folk music and dance festival in all of the Scandinavian countries, rekindling Finland's passion for folksy tunes and bringing folk music to many thousands of young people for the first time. The variety of music is large, from the iconic folk songs of Varttina, one of Finland's most famous folk bands who have spent 30 years together, to the new-blood of folk musician troupes who are pushing the boundaries of the genre, fusing soulful sounds with rock, gypsy, jazz and even salsa. The Finnish landscape – so often the anchor for the lyrics of its songs – hosts its folk tradition in grand style. On a rocky terrain that is amongst the oldest anywhere in the world, Finland boasts incredible granite formations created over two billion years ago. With translucent lakes, warm summer breezes, the scent of wildflowers and, of course, the mythical white nights, the hundreds of folk performances at Kaustinen, with its busking, dances and jam sessions, celebrate all that is unique about Finnish folk music as well as folk traditions from near and far. Thousands of amateur and professional musicians from around the world strike a common chord here every summer, with exciting international names in contemporary folk music adding to the mix. As well as bringing a Finnish regional theme into focus, the Kaustinen Folk Festival also centres on a world music theme, such as Mexican folk, the folk music of Greece or Croatian fiddle music.

In short, Kaustinen Folk Music Festival aims to cater for a variety of tastes, from Nordic to Irish folk music, together with plenty of influence from Africa and North America. With the compelling landscape as its backdrop, and Mother Nature running the light show, this is a world-beating vibrant celebration of folk in a country that truly adores the countryside. This is quintessential Finland at its most spellbinding, amongst horseback-riding, canoeing, rock-climbing and lush, low-lying plains. A legacy of the ice age that occurred about 10,000 years ago is a terrain peppered with glacial hollows now filled by thousands of sun-dappled lakes. Barbecuing, fishing, swimming and boating are favourite summer pastimes in Finland, where 450 avian species include many rarely encountered anywhere else in Europe. Newts, frogs, toads and lizards and almost 70 species of freshwater fish enjoy the flora, insects and pristine waters of the lakes in amongst moss, plants, ferns and lichen. Swathes of forests, berry bushes and flowering plants characterise the Finnish countryside where you will find 37 national parks freely accessible to the public all year round. In winter, this resplendent countryside is showcased under the glowing blue-green-yellow strobes of the Northern Lights while in summer, the endless bright-white sunshine blurs the boundaries between the fade of night and a dawning day.

Contacts:
Visit Finland
visitfinland.com

Music of Finland
musicfinland.fi

BERGEN, NORWAY

Norwegians feel about Edvard Grieg (1843–1907) the way that the British feel about William Shakespeare and Americans George Washington: he is a celebrated national icon. And Grieg's hometown of Bergen stirs up a similar passion from its patriotic population, as the bastion of many Norwegian cultural traditions. Whilst it celebrates the masters of the past in innumerable museums, book stores and galleries, Bergen is a lively student city full of the vibrant promise of youth. Founded more than 900 years ago, with its roots in the Viking Age and beyond, Bergen once formed the mid-point on the prosperous trade route between Norway and the rest of Europe. Whilst its trade role is no more, Bergen retains its cultural importance, hosting the International Festival each year – one of Norway's biggest events. Throughout the city there are constant reminders of the works of the Norwegian composer and pianist. Grieg is best known for his 'Piano Concerto in A minor' and *Peer Gynt*, which includes the magical compositions 'Morning Mood' and 'In the Hall of the Mountain King'. His enthusiasm for his compositions and his country enhanced Grieg's reputation with his fellow Norwegians and he was much respected for his entire career.

The house that is home to Bergen's Edvard Grieg Museum was the composer's private residence for 22 years. It was here that Grieg famously created many of his best-known works in a little hut set in his garden. Today the living museum replicates his home as it once was, complete with violins, books and personal effects. Furniture, furnishings, paints and artefacts date back to 1885 and Grieg appears to have dedicated himself to single-handedly creating a national identity for classical music in Norway, such was his flag-waving patriotism. In a letter to his American biographer, Henry Finck, Grieg once explained: '[the] traditional way of life of the Norwegian people, together with Norway's legends, Norway's history, Norway's natural scenery, stamped itself on my creative imagination from my earliest years'. He was desperately unhappy at school, suffering regularly at the hands of bullies after contracting tuberculosis, which left him with only one functioning lung. A chance meeting with composer Rikard Nordraak during a visit to Copenhagen in 1862 changed Grieg's life forever, teaching him that national pride could be expressed in musical terms to dramatic effect. Nordraak's premature death in 1866 encouraged Grieg to stage a concert of his own compositions, including some piano miniatures and the 'First Violin Sonata', which was greeted with riotous applause. In 1867 – against his family's better judgment – the composer married his cousin Nina Hagerup, a talented pianist with an enchanting singing voice that bewitched Grieg. The couple had a daughter, Alexandra, who died of meningitis. However, Grieg felt a flurry of inspiration, composing his first and most enduring masterpiece, the 'Piano Concerto in A minor'. It was to prove a total sensation, after which he bought the house in Bergen. Grieg flourished in Bergen, enjoying a highly productive and creative period in which he penned all his most critically acclaimed works. In the summer of 1906 he completed his final composition – the 'Four Psalms'. He felt weak and fatigued as he began to plan ahead for an autumn tour of Britain. Grieg and his wife had long enjoyed

Photo: Sveter

tremendous celebrity and continued to travel extensively around Europe, often spending time with internationally renowned composers such Tchaikovsky, Brahms and Liszt, where he was well-regarded for his sincerity and his work ethic. He earned a generous income from a vigorous schedule of recital tours and also served briefly as the music director of both the Bergen Symphony Orchestra and the Bergen Harmonien. However, Grieg was unable to keep up with the pace that was eventually to catch up with him. In 1907, an exhausted Grieg suffered a massive heart attack and died later in hospital. He was 64.

Today, as Norway's most famous composer, Grieg is heralded as one of the truly great late Romantics, whose music was infused with the pride, pageantry and folk tradition of his homeland. Daily matinée concerts (mid-May to late-September) and evening concerts each Sunday (mid-June to late-August) are staged locally in Bergen city centre with the museum offering guided tours throughout the summer too, at 11am each day. Busses leave the Tourist Information office in Bergen to Edvard Grieg's villa on the outskirts of the city (cost – adults NOK 250 / children NOK 100). After visiting the villa, there is plenty of time to explore the gardens and see the composer's hut overlooking the water. The tour includes the peaceful gravesite and a concert at the local chamber music hall, where one of Norway's leading pianists gives a 30-minute Grieg recital. Visitors are then ferried back to the city centre at 2pm. Tickets are sold at the Tourist Information office until 10.30am on the day. It is also possible to arrange tours around Grieg Hall, a high-tech concert venue named in honour of Bergen's musical hero, which earned fame as the host of the 1986 European Song Contest and has since been transformed into Norway's leading integrated culture hub.

Other Grieg-related events include a ten-week festival programme that celebrates his music at annual event MusicaNord, which takes place between June and September. It features orchestras from all over the world and draws crowds from far and wide, see: grieginbergen.com. Since its inception as Norway's first professional vocal ensemble in 2012, the Edvard Grieg Kor has performed widely to great acclaim, not just in its own right, but also as a core participant in the Bergen National Opera and Bergen Philharmonic choruses – tickets always sell out fast.

Contacts:
Bergen Tourism
visitbergen.com

Visit Norway
visitnorway.com

Grieg Museum
griegmuseum.no

SALZBURG, AUSTRIA

Salzburg may be home to Mozart and all things baroque, but for an astounding 70 per cent of visitors from overseas, it is *The Sound of Music* that lures them to the city. As the most successful musical film ever produced, *The Sound of Music* won five Oscars, and grossed more ticket sales than any other musical in history. Based on a book by Maria von Trapp published in 1949, *The Sound of Music* won fans after

Photo: Gerhard Mauracher

becoming a hit Rodgers & Hammerstein Broadway show. No one imagined that the cinema version would inspire millions of fans to dream of making a pilgrimage to Salzburg to see where it was filmed. However, today the city, with its fine old buildings, medieval streets, art museums, Mozart connections and pretty cafés serving delicious coffee and cake, welcome music-lovers from all over the world, keen to sing and dance in the footsteps of Julie Andrews, Christopher Plummer and seven chirpy children on the verdant mountains.

As a scenic location, Salzburg and the Austrian mountains offers breath-taking views with lush carpets of green curving over the foothills, meadows scattered with alpine flowers and rugged peaks under vast open skies. The sense of open space in which to breathe is joyfully freeing; no wonder Salzburg and its picturesque surrounding landscapes are a UNESCO World Heritage site. Using the numerous pictur-esque locations, director Robert Wise utilised the many facets of Salzburg throughout the entire film: though not that many native Austrians have watched it – in a bizarre twist, the movie wasn't on general release on home soil. In fact, few Austrians fully understand the enormous impact a film about music in the Salzburg mountains has on the world – even more than 50 years on. However, such was the demand, local tour companies began to offer day-trips – the response was overwhelming, and today visitors are spoilt for choice by the number of different excursions on a *Sound of Music* theme. Cross the River Salzach on the Mozartsteg footbridge; stroll around the horse fountain on Residenz Square; soak up the beauty of the scene made famous by the 'Do-Re-Mi' sequence in the meadow of Gschwandtanger, with a 900-year-old castle set on fir-clad slopes creating a breathtaking backdrop.

As you can imagine, bemused locals have grown used to prancing tourists swirling past the fountains, singing at the top of their lungs, skipping up and down the city's stone steps and patting a stone gnome on the head. Whilst not every scene was shot in Austria – some were cleverly replicated in Hollywood – Robert Wise juggled multiple locations in and around Salzburg and fully exploited its cinematic potential. Captain von Trapp's home, for example, is a combination of two different mansions – Schloss Frohnburg (now a music school) and Schloss Leopoldskron. There's also the gardens where Liesl had her first kiss – a prime spot for tourist photographs in the parklands of Schloss Hellbrunn. Book in advance and this romantic setting can be used as the perfect place for a marriage proposal, complete with music (of course). A short drive away is the lakeside resort of Mondsee, where on her marriage day Maria walked down the long aisle of the baroque St Michael's basilica to become the Captain's bride. After the proposal, this is where *Sound of Music* die-hards from every corner of the world come to say 'I do' – the scenery is magical: emerald-coloured springy alpine meadows edged by the spires and steeples of Salzburg with visions of Maria twirling fabulously beneath a sunny sky. If the people of Salzburg cringe inwardly at the folksy melody and corny lyrics of *The Sound of Music*, they hide it well. At the lake where the unforgettable boating scene took place and at the Nonnberg Convent where Maria lived as a young nun, the guides are enthusiastic – bursting into song with visitors when the urge to sing 'Edelweiss' is impossible to resist.

Set in Austria in the 1930s, the story centres on a young woman named Maria who is failing miserably in her attempts to become a nun. When the Navy captain Georg Von Trapp asks the convent for a governess that can handle his seven mischievous children, Maria is given the job. The Captain's wife is dead, he is often away, and the children are unhappy and resentful of the governesses that their father keeps hiring. They have seen each one off in succession, so when Maria arrives the children try the same trick. However, her kindness, understanding and sense of fun soon draw them to her and Maria brings some much-needed joy into all their lives – the Captain included. Eventually he and Maria find themselves falling in love, even though Georg is already engaged to a Baroness and Maria is still a postulant. The romance makes them both start questioning the decisions they have made. Their personal conflicts soon become overshadowed, however, by world events – Austria is about to come under the control of Germany. The Captain may soon find himself drafted, but Maria continues to sing with the children to keep spirits high. Of course, there was a healthy dollop of artistic license in telling the true story of Maria, but when 20th Century Fox put on a special screening for the family they were thrilled with the emotion and power of the interpretation.

During the filming of the movie more than 250 crew members spent months in Salzburg, bringing the city to the attention of the world when *The Sound of Music* premiered in 1965. Now a film with global cult status, the tremendous success of the von Trapp family continues to live on in the hearts and minds of everyone that visits Salzburg. Being here, on the resplendent mountain backdrop, in amongst the historical and cinematic landmarks, provides a lasting *Sound of Music* memory. Enjoy a traditional Austrian lunch on the shores of Lake Fuschl or Lake Wolfgang, where the panoramic shots and scenes of the picnic were filmed. Salzburg is also home to a number of performances and shows with a *Sound of Music* connection, including a musical in the city's century-old Salzburg Marionette Theatre (see: marionetten.at), and a Sound of Salzburg Dinner Show that combines songs from the film with a three-course meal (see: soundofsalzburg.info). At the Villa Trapp, non-guests can book a 45-minute guided tour (villa-trapp.cc).

Contacts:
Villa Trapp
villa-trapp.cc

Salzburgland Tourism
salzburgerland.com

Salzburg Music Tours
salzburg.info

ASIA

SEOUL, SOUTH KOREA

Visit Asia and it is almost impossible to escape the phenomena of K-pop – a genre of catchy chart songs that dominates the airwaves – wherever you are. In the Western world, most people's knowledge of South Korean music ends at 'Gangnam Style'. However, the musical subculture dedicated to South Korean pop music is much more than a single catchy dance tune. Upbeat melodies, happy bubblegum lyrics and fiendishly contagious hooks are the dynamos powering the rise of K-pop. Only the catchiest tunes sung by the most memorable K-pop idols resonate from South Korea out to the wider world, but those that do rack up massive sales as well as millions of fans across the planet. An album from EXO, South Korea's biggest boy-band, was the fifth biggest-selling album in the world in 2015. Slick, synchronised dance moves become the latest craze on every dance floor with K-pop videos attracting over 10 million views on YouTube within a few short hours of their release. Concert tickets are snapped up by an eager public within a matter of minutes of going on the market. Swept up in a tsunami of cute lyrics, pretty faces and heartthrob dance moves, fans are slavishly devoted to the K-pop cult, buying each and every CD, DVD and MP3 download. The lyrics and personal lives of their idols are scrutinised and each iconic fashion style copied with forensic precision. 'It's more than just music,' admits 25-year-old Tae Min from the city of Seoul, 'it's my whole life.'

Of course, almost everyone in the world knows of veteran South Korean pop singer Psy: the force behind the viral worldwide megahit 'Gangnam Style'. Clocking up well over 2 billion views on YouTube since 2012, 'Gangnam Style' smashed the Guinness World Record for being the most liked video on YouTube to date. Psy achieved what every K-pop star dreams of: to top the music charts across Asia, North America and Europe, and be played in every household worldwide. As the first ever South Korean musician to achieve such success, Psy proved a force to be reckoned with as a true global phenomenon – even though he doesn't possess K-pop's perfect good looks.

The emergence of K-pop can be traced back to the mid-late 1990s, when groups such as Fin.K.L, g.o.d, H.O.T., Sechs Kies, and S.E.S. began to notch up chart hits throughout Asia. K-pop stars are nurtured via a talent agency 'apprenticeship' – the tried and tested strategy for transforming girl groups, boy bands and solo artists into money-spinning musical icons. New talent is scouted, fully subsidised and coached for two years in a bid for stardom – conservative estimates suggest the basic cost is at least $500,000. Voices are honed, bodies sculpted and dance moves perfected. They are even put through language school so that they can successfully promote hit records on TV and radio chat shows in countries all around the world. Solo artist Taeyang and girl group 2NE1 are fine examples of this formulaic approach to K-pop stardom. Both dominated the Asian charts before being launched into foreign markets. Today, as much-loved media darlings, Taeyang and 2NE1 and their feel-good songs have clocked up numerous hits across the United States, Canada and Australia. They have followed in the footsteps of the Wonder Girls, who became the first Korean singers to achieve a place on the US Billboard Hot 100 Chart with their sing-along single, 'Nobody'.

Like many other K-pop artists, these acts have increasingly worked with producers outside of Korea to achieve a greater international success, including collaborations with Kanye West and will.i.am. Yet most cite boy band H.O.T. (High-five Of Teenagers) as the very first K-pop band to hit the scene. H.O.T. debuted in September 1996 – the year that the term K-pop was first coined. They burst into the charts with their fresh-faced square jaws, flawless complexions and high-energy music at a time when pop was dominated by ballad-singing solo artists and singer-songwriters. H.O.T. defined youthful perfection with their model looks, cutting-edge style and banging dance routines. Within a few short weeks of charting, the five band members – Kangta, Moon HeeJun, Tony Ahn, Jang WooHyuk, and Lee JaeWon – were worshiped by legions of adoring fans and for five years (1996–2001) achieved a tremendous level of success and popularity that ensured they were the most instantly

Photo: Korea.net / Korean Culture and Information Service (Jeon Han)

recognised celebrity faces in Korea. Even once they had disbanded, H.O.T. continued to retain its fame as the icon of a generation and the inspiration behind future K-pop stars Shinhwa, TVXQ, Super Junior, SHINee, EXO and more. Today former H.O.T. band members remain active in the entertainment industry as TV presenters, record label executives, actors and more.

In South Korea's capital Seoul, the district around the city's Hongik University has become something of a hub for K-pop tourists with its fashionable coffee shops, eateries, flea markets, buzzing bars and neon-lit clubs. Numerous K-pop videos and Korean TV teen dramas are shot in the streets that fan out around the university and in the haunts in which young Koreans enjoy dancing and singing to their favourite tunes by snake-hipped boy bands in. Local hoteliers report that around 30 per cent of guests are drawn to the district by their interest in K-pop and the variants of the genre that incorporate rap, rock and techno. Old-school K-pop is huge in the bars around Hongik University so expect to bop to 1990s chart bands Deux and S.E.S. Some of the clubs run regular K-pop competitions for band merchandise and memorabilia, while a recent university poll to establish the most highly anticipated fantasy K-pop couple resoundingly favoured Apink's Chorong and Exo's Suho. One of the biggest party nights in the clubs around the university took place when first-generation K-pop band S.E.S. announced their comeback with a brand new reunion album for January 2017. Glasses clinked, crowds shrieked and hollered as DJs played S.E.S. mega-mixes into the wee small hours.

Contacts:
K-pop fan zone
kpopmap.com

Korea Tourism
visitkorea.or.kr

BEIJING, CHINA

Chinese opera – together with Greek tragic-comedy and Indian Sanskrit opera – are the world's three oldest dramatic art forms. It has entertained for thousands of years and during its golden age it held a special place in the hearts and minds of the Chinese people. Yet the opera and its legions of adoring fans have faced horrific, dark times too.

The first known opera was staged during the Song Dynasty (960–1279) and underwent a huge period of rich productive change in the Yuan Dynasty under emperor Kublai Khan. However this proud operatic heritage was almost lost forever during the mid-20th century. After initially encouraging the arts, intellectualism and operatic tradition to flourish as part of the 'Hundred Flowers Campaign' (1956–1957), the Communist regime of the People's Republic of China suddenly clamped down on the intellectuals and artists who had put themselves forward. Between July and December more than 300,000 people had been labelled 'rightists'. The luckiest of these were shamed and punished by public criticism. Others were executed or interned indefinitely in labour camps. Some simply 'disappeared'.

During the Cultural Revolution (1966–1976) the very existence of Chinese opera and other traditional arts was threatened as 'one of the old ways of thinking' that the regime sought to eradicate entirely. In fact it was an attack on the Beijing opera and a notable operatic composer that

signalled the start of the Cultural Revolution. Composers and scriptwriters were arrested, opera troupes disbanded and the performance of opera outlawed – apart from eight 'model operas' that had been personally sanctioned by Madame Jiang Qing for political and cultural content. The result was bland and uninspiring.

However, in 1976 Chinese opera regained its place within the national repertoire and the tradition was revived – with new students trained by the very same veteran performers who were once detained by the authorities for their art. Since then, traditional operas have been freely performed though some of the newer, more modern works have been subjected to censorship. Today, more than 30 forms of Chinese opera are performed regularly throughout the country in tearooms, restaurants, civic buildings and outdoor stages. With its distinctive sound and unique dialectical musical style, it is derived from a mix of folk songs, dances, story-telling and poetry. Over time it has gradually combined music, art and literature into one performance, using traditional instruments such as the *erhu*, gong and lute. To the Western ear, the sound is utterly extraordinary and seems to follow a musical arrangement quite unlike any other. Yet the lyrics are beautifully crafted in clearly distinct literary styles, such as *zaju*, popularised during the Yuan Dynasty. The Chinese consider it a privilege to listen to the poetry of opera: it's nostalgic; it's proud and above all it's a pleasure.

Apart from the music, Chinese opera is also famous for the artistry it uses in its traditional facial make-up, an age-old craft that is characterised by exaggerated designs and practiced by highly-trained theatrical artists. Each colour used reflects the personality, role, and fate of a character – for example a red face tells the audience the actor is loyal and brave; a black face indicates valour; lies and deceit are depicted by the colour yellow, with gold and silver faces reflecting mystery. Operas also incorporate spectacular acrobatics and circus-style effects, using fire, swords and physical distortion. Over the course of its 800-year history, Chinese opera has evolved into many different regional varieties that use local traits and accents – and today there are as many different styles of regional opera as there are days of the year.

Kunqu opera, which originated around Jiangsu Province, is a typical ancient opera style and features gentleness and clearness. This enabled it to be ranked as a Masterpiece of the Oral and Intangible Heritage of Humanity by UNESCO. *Qinqiang* opera from Shaanxi, is known for its loudness and wildness, and Yu opera, Yue opera, and *Huangmei* opera are all very enjoyable. Beijing opera, the best-known Chinese opera style, was formed from the mingling of these regional styles and was established by travelling opera troupes during the Qing Dynasty (1644–1911), in the 55th year reigned by the Emperor Qianlong (1790). As it has a long history in the Imperial Court, Beijing opera has developed differently from other operas. Themes are broader, although usually are historical and characters more complex (there are four main types of roles: *Sheng, Dan, Jing* and *Chou*). Costumes are sumptuous and brightly-coloured with long gowns in gorgeous silks and satins and the stage makeup places even greater emphasis on definition, using bats, swallows or butterfly wings for eyebrows and oversized eyes and cheeks, nose and mouth. Armour, headdresses, boots and shoes are richly embellished regardless of which of the Beijing opera's 3,800 plays is being staged. Musically the Beijing opera is reliant on a single-skin drum, percussion block and large gong together with a number of bow-played string instruments of varied high-pitched ranges, such as the two-stringed *jing erhu*.

As the music was created before electrical amplification and microphones, performers needed to project their voice as far, and as powerfully, as possible. Musicians (collectively known as *chang*) also played their instruments with skilful force in order for the sound to resonate. The result is a pounding dialogue combined with piercing high-pitched nasal song, daring fight scenes, comedy, slow motion acting, high-paced martial arts and acrobatics, powerful narratives and drama.

For Western tastes, one of the easiest Chinese operas to appreciate is a modern story called 'Rapper Face' as it cleverly combines traditional Beijing opera singing and rhythm with easy-to-follow pop music, martial arts, and well-crafted lyrics. Each act contains equal proportions of *chang* (singing), *nian* (speaking), *zuo* (acting) and *da* (fighting) – using a common tune that accurately expresses the feelings of the dramatic persona. Some of the best Chinese opera performances can be found at the Liyuan Theatre, the home of Beijing opera, where a pair of large LED screens flash a translation of the lyrics and the plot to the non-Chinese. Arrive early to pick up cheap last-minute tickets and you'll be able to watch as the cast paint their faces and put on their costumes from your seat.

Contacts:
Liyuan Theatre
liyuantheatreopera.com

China National Tourist Organisation
cnto.org

FUJI ROCK FESTIVAL, JAPAN

For the fans that gather there once a year, the Fuji Rock Festival is utterly magical. Sure, the quality of the line-up is second to none. But it's more than that. The setting – a jagged mountain spine peppered with steam-shrouded, bubbling hot geysers under glowing red skies – must be one of the most mesmerising gig locations ever. Forget the chaos of European festivals, Fuji Rock is as orderly as a coach tour: clean toilets that work, amazing food, no queues to buy beer, an incredibly friendly crowd – and that's all before a single chord has been played. Mixing the best in British, American and Japanese indie, dance and world music with 100,000 people over three long summer days, the festival has attracted massive acts like Radiohead, Oasis, Red Hot Chili Peppers, Beck, Foo Fighters, Beastie Boys and Roxy Music, as well as crowd-pleasers the Violators, Floating Points and Toe. People describe being drawn to this great musical gathering with a mountain view, just to be there, soak up the atmosphere, be cool and hang out.

Since the first Fuji Rock was staged in 1997, Japan's annual festival has become a well-kept secret with music-lovers across the globe. Though it moved to the Naeba Ski Resort in 1999, the Fuji Rock Festival retains its name in honour of the slopes of the mountain on which it was first staged. The first year of the event has earned its place in festival folklore amongst Fuji Rock veterans. A typhoon hit the site on Mount Fuji, on the first day during the Red Hot Chili Peppers' headline set. They played on, determinedly, through a storm despite lead singer Anthony Kiedis having a broken arm. The weather had been warm and dry in the run up to the event,

Photo: Kevin Utting

so festival goers were poorly prepared for torrential rain and strong winds. Crowds of people needed medical attention for hypothermia and the second day was cancelled. Tokyo's waterfront was chosen as the venue for the second year but the searing heat of mid-summer in the city was too much to bear for some. For year three, the festival returned to the relative coolness of the mountains when a new home was found in Naeba in the Niigata Prefecture – miles and miles away from the original Mount Fuji site. Thankfully, since that disastrous first year, the festival can boast the best of smooth running, with the schedule running Friday to Sunday.

Today the event welcomes more than 200 Japanese and international musicians to the breathtaking scenery of Japan's oh-so picturesque Yuzawa area. On arrival, festival goers are transported to the top of the mountain by the Dragondola – the longest gondola lift in the world. As it glides slowly upwards, the views become increasingly more spellbinding, offering an unbroken sweeping panorama across the entire festival site. With seven main stages supported by a host of smaller stages scattered across the site, the main draw is the Green Stage, which has capacity for almost 50,000 spectators. Performance areas are connected by pathways that meander across beautiful hilly terrain, through forests and over sparkling streams. More than 30 eateries producing high-quality foods from all over the globe offer everything from Mexican tacos, Italian pasta dishes, sushi, British fish and chips and gourmet burgers. For the night owls that rave in the Red Marquee all night there is even a ground coffee bar that serves breakfast from 4am. Rubbish is minimal, food is from a sustainable source and everything is recycled – a very good reason why the Fuji Rock Festival has been hailed 'the cleanest festival in the world'.

Early bird arrivals can start partying the night before the official start of the festival at a free opening party. The highlight is undoubtedly the traditional Japanese folk dance (*Bon Odori*) in which ancestors are honoured, remembered and praised for all they have done. These typically Buddhist celebrations also centre on the ongoing role the ancestors continue to enjoy today. Dancers wear Japanese kimono, *yukata* or *happi* coats and there are also *taiko* and martial arts performances, craft exhibits and artisan demonstrations. A free shuttle bus links the local transport hub and outlying accommodation in the town of Yuzawa, and runs until 2am each night. Alternatively, there is a campsite on a golf course next to the festival site that can accommodate 17,000 festival goers together with car parking. For city-slickers and international visitors, Yuzawa is a straightforward hour-and-a-half train ride from Tokyo.

In an era when Glastonbury tickets sell out at a price that could fund a small mortgage, Fuji Rock is a true showcase of authentic alternative music that manages to attract such high calibre names as Muse, Noel Gallagher, Manic Street Preachers, Basement Jaxx, Belle and Sebastian, Outkast, The Cure, Nine Inch Nails, Radiohead, Franz Ferdinand, Lou Reed, Feeder, Primal Scream, Green Day, Sparks, Jarvis Cocker, Kings of Leon, Groove Armada, Kaiser Chiefs, Brian Eno, Ocean Colour Scene, Placebo, Stereo MCs, Sonic Youth and Weezer – seemingly with effortless ease. Fuji Rock remains proud of its refusal to court the relentless consumerism of many of the world's other big weekend festivals. From high up in the mountains surrounding Niigata, cloaked in a fine silvery summer mist, the dance floors and mosh pits are powered by solar energy. Stallholders sell inexpensive trinkets or are there to champion environmental causes, ensuring the market place section of Fuji Rock is rich in free spirit feel-good vibes: it feels like a charitable, neighbourly eco-community. Walkways lit by disco balls and illuminated pink flamingos lead to palatial toilet blocks with flushing loos, hot showers and changing rooms. There is even a women-only area set around a marquee tent, with a restaurant, spa and chill-out zone, together with that elusive festival elixir – free-flowing hot water.

Contacts:
Fuji Rock
fujirock.com

Japan Tourism
seejapan.co.uk

HAMAMATSU, JAPAN

If you own a Yamaha organ, a Suzuki amp, a Kawai piano or a sleek-necked Tokai guitar, the chances are it has been made in Hamamatsu: a Japanese city that is almost entirely devoted to music. From a vibrant music education scene, musical R&D fraternity and famous musical instrument manufacturers to a roll-call of brilliant musicians that perform every year at Hamamatsu's various World Federation of International Music competitions, the city in western Shizuoka has music at its core. It is also where you'll find Japan's prestigious Museum of Musical Instruments, a unique institution offering a view on humanity and culture through an exceptional collection of musical instruments from around the world. Workshops, concerts, studios and production companies in Hamamatsu have also been critically acclaimed and training courses for professional musicians and artists, as well as activities preserving and promoting traditional performing arts, are offered throughout the city. The Hamamatsu Academy of Music, for example, implements wide-ranging music-related projects, raises public interest in music and supports future performers, instructors and concert hosts; and the Shizuoka University of Art and Culture offers courses in music management, which includes instruction on planning and producing concerts, as well as in concert hall management. But it isn't all about major institutions and corporations. Hamamatsu is also home to independent, family-owned flute-makers, piano-tuners, repair shops and manuscript printers in its side-streets and displays of hand-made pianos are a common sight in the concourse of the railway station.

1897 was a seminal year for Hamamatsu's musical history, for it was when Torakusu Yamaha, a local reed organ repairman, decided to try his hand at building his own organ. His prototype worked, and he soon had an order book that grew in size. His business – now known as Yamaha – was soon producing strings, brass and woodwinds as well as other orders, which put Hamamatsu squarely on the map. Before long, Yamaha was joined by piano-maker Kawai, Suzuki Musical Instruments and Tokai Guitars. Today more than 90 per cent of Western-style musical instruments produced in Japan are made in Hamamatsu. A high proportion of business start-ups here are connected to the music industry, such as promoters, management companies, concert organisers and musical publishers. There's plenty to do, see and hear, relating to Hamamatsu's musical industry with both Suzuki and Yamaha offering visitor tours and plenty of museums and exhibitions. Many of the small, bespoke instrument craftsmen offer personalised tours too by appointment,

for example the Hikosaka Koto Shamisen Shop (tel: 053-452-5566; e-mail wagakki@dream.com). Anyone who lives and breathes music will enjoy the privilege of spending an hour with the creative talent behind traditionally made Japanese musical instruments. Makoto Hikosaka, the son of the shop's founder, is extremely knowledgeable about the history of the wood-and-string *koto* and *shamisen*, which were once crafted using thick, ribbed strings of silk but are now made using stronger synthetic materials. Visitors can watch him restringing a *koto*: knotting and threading and looping with deft precision until the 13 strings are accurately in place. To tune, Hikosaka then carefully knots each string in succession, until the right pitch is achieved. Then he ties them tightly together, tucking them into the *koto*'s hollow frame before outlining the history of the shop, which opened just after the end of the Second World War. Today one of the best-selling instruments is the *tsuzumi* drum, a hand-held percussion instrument that is used in traditional Japanese theatre and folk music parades. With its bar-bell shape, the *tsuzumi* drum is always played at festivals throughout Japan, and it has a distinctive tone that can be changed by pulling the cords around it tighter or loosening them off.

At the Hamamatsu Museum of Musical Instruments, a 45-storey landmark tower just on the other side of the city's railway station, a collection of 1,300 musical instruments from all over the world range from the usual to the rare and downright odd. This massive exhibit scales several floors and tells the story of how instruments were influenced by different cultures as they crossed trade routes and human migration paths. Displays on different countries range from European brass instruments and South American flutes to drums from Oceania and Africa. In each zone, headsets are provided so that visitors can hear the instruments' sound when being played. Exhibition boards (in Japanese and English) detail facts and figures about Hamamatsu's musical roots. There is a huge collection of organs, pianos (of every size and shape) and harpsichords, from duet pianos with keyboards at opposite ends of a single case to a twin-keyboarded grand piano. Part of the UNESCO Creative City Network, Hamamatsu became a 'City of Music' in December 2014.

All around the Hamamatsu Museum of Musical Instruments venue there are nice places to stroll amongst music-inspired art, such as Waclaw Szymanowski's haunting sculpture of Frederic Chopin. Located about midway between Tokyo and Osaka, near the centre of Honshu, Hamamatsu is popular with weekenders keen to sense the mountains and the sea. 'Japan's City of Music' doesn't just claim the monopoly on music, it also boasts some beautiful coastal scenery at Nakatajima Sakyu: an expansive stretch of rolling dunes that reach down to the Pacific Ocean. From early summer to autumn, loggerhead turtles come to lay their eggs underneath legendary sunsets. There's also a kite-flying festival here to raise awareness of marine conservation.

Meanwhile, throughout the day, the Hamamatsu Museum hosts a series of mini-concerts for the public. It could be a hush-making performance of Chopin pieces played on a 19th-century Pleyel piano – or a show-stopping showcase of electronic musical technologies using a suite of synths. Sometimes it may be percussion, or guitar, but given the pedigree of Hamamatsu it is the keyboards that are usually the stars. A hands-on room, where visitors can let kids run wild, encourages them to pluck banjo strings, shake giant maracas and bang out a tune on a colour-coded Caribbean steel drum.

Contacts:

Hamamatsu Museum of Musical Instruments
gakkihaku.jp

Hamamatsu Music Tours
hamamatsu-daisuki.net

Hamamatsu Tour Guide
inhamamatsu.com

RISHIKESH, INDIA

As a vast expanse of land, India is a complex patchwork of diverse cultures that as many pilgrims flock to discover as in the age of the great ancient civilisation itself. As the home of the oldest religious pilgrimage tradition in the world, the practice of 'discovery' is deeply embedded in the cultural psyche of the entire subcontinent: be it the search for religious divinity, sacred peace or a heightened sense of spirit. In each of these pursuits music has long played a vital role, from the chanting of the Vedic period and the song of the *Mahabharata* to the rhythmic breathing of the *Puranas* as the bridge is sought between heaven and earth. Places, people, song and study are all central to Buddhist, Sikh and Hindu beliefs and with the great lakes, the mighty Ganges River, sacred Bodhi trees and the snow-covered reaches of the lofty Garhwal Himalayas, India is rich in spirituality, scripture, shrines, melody and mythology. In the northern reaches of the country, the town of Rishikesh sprang to worldwide fame during the late 1960s when the

Beatles sought yogic guidance from Maharishi Mahesh Yogi. Though it had been a magnet for spiritual seekers for over a thousand years, the Beatles thrust Rishikesh and its exquisite forested landscape on the fast-flowing Ganges into the global spotlight. Today it styles itself as the 'Yoga Capital of the World'. From the tinkling chimes of temple bells on a scented breeze and the vivid hues of brightly-coloured petals, to musky incense, fire offerings, banging gongs, the distinctive pluck and twang of an Indian sitar and low hum of ritual chants, Rishikesh offers all kinds of yoga, meditation and mindfulness classes. The Beatles chose this auspicious spiritual town as a place in which to deepen their transcendental meditative understanding, arriving to a blaze of publicity in February 1968. What followed was *The White Album*, and a lasting change in how the world viewed India and the yogic tradition.

Today, Rishikesh is a mix of preserved and dilapidated structures with strong Beatles connections, many of which are now riddled with tree roots as the surrounding forest attempts to claim it back. Paul McCartney, George Harrison, Ringo Starr and John Lennon were going through a troubled phase before deciding on a three-month stay at the retreat (*ashram*) in Rishikesh. They booked in for an advanced course of meditation at the eighteen-acre ashram in a bid that it would help glue the band back together and provide some fresh inspiration for their songs. During their stay here, the band penned more than 40 songs, eighteen of which are featured on *The White Album*, including 'Dear Prudence', 'Ob-La-Di, Ob-La-Da', 'The Continuing Story of Bungalow Bill', 'Back in the USSR', and 'I'm So Tired'. Two songs appeared on the *Abbey Road* album, and others were used for various solo projects. 'Everybody's Got Something to Hide Except Me and My Monkey', and 'Sexy Sadie' were

Photo: Aleksandr Zykov

reputed to have been written in reference to rumours that Maharishi Mahesh Yogi had groped a female guest, actress Mia Farrow, during her stay there.

The Beatles' Ashram, as it has come to be called, was abandoned in the 1970s before being taken over by the local forestry commission in 2003. It has continued to remain a big draw for Beatles fans around the world – a much less obvious choice than, say, Liverpool or London and you can spot where pilgrims have scaled the walls or bribed the guard to allow them to spend time walking in the footsteps of their musical heroes. In and around the retreat, there are steady streams of loincloth-clad travellers slowly plodding the town's hot, dusty streets to reach the banks of the sacred Ganges, which sweeps majestically through the town and out onto the great Indian plains. Here, on the steps that lead down to the water, gurus and yogic followers participate in daily prayers and fire worship. These rituals, combined with the classical music and philosophy of India, had a career-changing effect on the Beatles, who became fascinated by Indian culture and its traditional music and instruments. Though they first met the Maharishi Mahesh Yogi in London in 1967, when the group attended one of his lectures, at the time, nobody guessed that the association would lead to the Beatles' highest-selling and arguably most polarising album to date: a body of work so incredibly different from anything the Fab Four had done before.

The Beatles' Ashram is set at the end of a loose-stone track behind a set of huge iron gates overlooking the Ganges River. Daily rituals create magical moods: first the cymbals, then the drums and then finally the singing begins, echoing the rhythm of the river. Days start early with yoga and meditation and learning how to pursue a simple, clean, healthy way of life – this silent time is important as it allows you to stretch, breathe and contemplate. The diet is vegetarian, the living arrangements communal, and at night candles are lit and sent down the river in leaf baskets as an after-dark ritual. It is also customary for devotees to take a dip in the Ganges, bobbing up and down under the water three times before cupping the water and imbibing it.

Most foreign visitors do like the Beatles and fly into New Delhi before transferring to Rishikesh the next day. The Fab Four stayed at the Oberoi Hotel and enjoyed a day of full-on shopping Indian-style, buying artefacts from antique shops and Indian instruments from Rikhi Ram & Sons on New Delhi's Connaught Circle. By the time the Beatles had left India, the influence of the country was highly visible – in their facial hair, their clothes, their vocabulary and their music. Numerous songs by the band have a telltale Indian influence, including the sound of the instruments the band purchased in Delhi. Forty years on and *The White Album* still prompts great debate and divided opinion. In 2001, the TV network VH1 named it 'the 11th greatest album ever' and in 2003, *Rolling Stone* ranked it number ten in its list of the 500 greatest albums of all time. In 2006, the album was chosen by *TIME* magazine as one of the 100 best albums of all time. What is undisputed is that this double Beatles album puts a heady mix of rock, pop and blues together in its 30 songs – twelve written by John, twelve written by Paul, four written by George, one written by Ringo and a sound collage written by John with help from George and Yoko. Dark and sinister at times, at others so bouncy it is ludicrous, with several occasions when the meaning is, quite simply, unfathomable, *The White Album* adds fire to the rumours surrounding John Lennon's obsession with the number 9: the album's second-longest track, at just over seven minutes is 'Revolution 9', a strange track that is much debated; he was born on 9 October 1940; his son was born on 9 October 1975; he wrote the song '#9 Dream' on *Walls and Bridges*, which was released on the ninth month of '74 and reached/peaked at number nine on the US charts and he was killed in the early hours of the morning of the 9 December 1980.

On *The White Album*, the Beatles embraced new musical ideas and applied their life experiences to their art, from political agitation to parody and tribute as part of a period of great self-discovery. The odd switches in tone from childish delight to fiendish paranoia are quite unlike anything else that came out of the rock era. It is hailed as a masterpiece by many, but criticised as the work of four solo artists on one album by others. What is certain is that *The White Album* has a truckload of great songs on it that were accomplished after a time experiencing the traditional ways of Eastern asceticism, which either dispelled cynicism or fuelled it in claims that meditation would achieve world peace. John, Paul, George and Ringo were accompanied by their partners in India, namely Cynthia Lennon, actress Jane Asher (McCartney's then girlfriend), Pattie Boyd Harrison and Maureen Starkey as well as singer Donovan. Together they spent time meditating, resting, writing songs and attending the Maharishi's lectures, or having private and group sessions with him on the roof of his bungalow. On one dusky-pink evening, a flight of 40 or 50 beautiful emerald-green parrots landed dramatically in a nearby tree and glimmered like jewels in the evening light – a dreamy scene accompanied by the gentle sitar, mellow and serene with the shadows of the mountainous jungle as a backdrop. It was the perfect prelim to the intensity of the meditation sessions with the Maharishi that night.

Some fans will visit the Cavern Club on 10 Mathew Street, Liverpool in the UK (the venue for the band's first gig) or

Abbey Road in London (where the band famously recorded almost all of their studio material and where the famous road-crossing can be found from the 1969 album cover for *Abbey Road*). Only the most adventurous will follow the Fab Four to the Himalayan foothills. However, it is here that you can feel the influences that formed a watershed moment in the history of the Beatles. Today, it remains a wonderful place to relax and unwind among nature as the lyrics of 'Across the Universe' swirl around in your mind.

Contacts:
Rishikesh Tourism
rishikeshtourism.in

Heritage Music and Dance Tours of India
india-tourism.net

MUMBAI, INDIA

The unmistakable sweet songs that form the soundtrack of Bollywood's movies scale every possible human emotion from elation and love to tragic heartbreak. A swirl of strings evokes pain, yearning and love in all its melodious wonder, while a trilling high-pitched female vocal soars up into the heavens. Ethereal, effortless and utterly flawless, the male vocals are also romance-rich, though deep and rounded to draw a clear distinction between the genders. Bollywood still retains the wholesome themes of yore such as the forbidden joys of star-crossed lovers who declare they'll die in each other's arms. Innocent dream-sequence montages

Photo: Skip

ooze purity and charisma, as a charming musical ode to the glory of love.

Unlike Hollywood, Bollywood movies have music as an integral part of the narrative, with the score as important as the script. In fact, a Bollywood story destined for the silver screen often has its music created at the point of conception, using the voices of singers like Kishore Kumar, Kumar Sanu, Asha Bhosle and Shreya Ghoshal. Often it is the music that draws people to the cinema and it is the music that people fall in love with when they watch the film. One of the biggest musical talents in India is A. R. Rahman – the dynamo behind some of the most phenomenal Bollywood music: all pre-recorded, honey-toned tracks sung by playback singers and lip-synced by the actors in the film. Not that playback singers hide from the limelight – far from it; they receive major billing on cast lists and credits, and attract huge numbers of fans. Lavish budgets ensure the music is created with high production values and the very best classical, instrumental and orchestral works – a level of investment that often means that the music has a longer shelf-life than the movie itself.

Bollywood mixes marriage songs, oldies, patriotic music and meditation chants with dance beats and power ballad treatments to create a 'pop opera', capturing the high emotion and echoing the narration of the film. A. R. Rahman – nicknamed the 'Mozart of Madras' – is a maestro of Bollywood music, who expertly expresses passion, heartbreak, joy and violence using voices, notes and chords. As an Academy Award-winner who also has Grammy, BAFTA and National Film Awards as well as Golden Globes to his name, Rahman is part of an industry that produces more than 1,000 films every year and has an audience of 3.6 billion (half the population of the world). *Slumdog Millionaire*'s

'Jai Ho' – a wonderfully catching A. R. Rahman song that crossed into mainstream pop charts and still continues to be sold worldwide to this day – epitomises the musical potential of Hindi music. The 2008 film, directed by Danny Boyle and written by Simon Beaufoy, was filmed in India and had its score carefully woven into the script.

As the so-called City of Dreams, Mumbai is India's centre of melodrama, music and entertainment, and has been since the 1930s, when the output was still around 200 films a year. Though the quality, cinematography, story lines and technical skills of the filmmaking industry were fairly rudimentary when Bollywood cinema began, 21st-century investment has taken Indian cinema to great heights. Box office successes in India and overseas are immense, with celluloid impacting the Indian economy by billions of dollars and affecting all sections of society by imparting news and social trends. Technicolor themes often rely on stereotypical backdrops, such as leafy tea plantations in glossy emerald hues, comfort over a cup of Darjeeling chai, strutting peacocks, prowling tigers and the handsome towers of the majestic Taj Mahal.

Today there are several key locations in India that are favourites for video shoots of Bollywood songs, such as Fatehour Sikri, a UNESCO World Heritage Site an hour from Agra, used for the song 'Do Dil'. The song 'Bholi Bhali Ladki' from the movie *Sabse Bada Khiladi* was entirely shot in Jaipur's Birla Mandir, while Victoria Terminus in Mumbai and the Victoria Memorial Hall in Kolkata are stars of dozens of musical pieces by Bollywood's hottest stars. Another popular landscape with a number of musical scenes are the many hill stations in India, such as Srinagar in Kashmir, Shimla in Himachal Pradesh, Darjeeling in West Bengal and Wayanad in Kerala where classic songs, such as 'Yahoo', set against snow-capped mountains and 'Yeh Chaand Sa Roshan Chehra' on India's famous Dal Lake, have enraptured musical fans with beautiful sentiment and yearning on a backdrop of resplendent Indian countryside. Known as the Jewel in the Crown, Dal Lake is cherished by the citizens of Srinagar – and beyond. Fed by the fast-flowing Jhelum River, and edged by brightly-coloured wildflowers, Dal Lake forms part of a bird-scattered natural wetland that is famous for its floating gardens, rich in lotus flowers that blossom during the months of July and August. Created during the Mughal era, Dal Lake is a byword for unparalleled natural beauty in the hearts and minds of Kashmiris. Filmmakers have shot over twenty films in and around the famous lily-topped body of water, but it is probably most famous as the tranquil setting for Shashi Kapoor's tear-jerking lament about failed romance in *Jab Jab Phool Khile*.

Contacts:
Bollywood Music Tours
bollywoodtourpackage.com

Bollywood Music and Dance Tour
bollywoodtours.in

Mumbai Magic
mumbaimagic.com

AUSTRALASIA

THE SOLOMON ISLANDS

The breathy, ethereal sound of a wooden panpipe is like a sweet breeze: wispily fragile, yet powerful with a hidden force. To listen to panpipe music is to connect to the deep, native roots of an ancient culture. It is more than a sound; more than music even. It is an echo of the past. Anthropology studies have helped us to understand the important story-telling role music has played in the traditions of indigenous peoples. In the Solomon Islands, an archipelago of 992 tropical isles and atolls, scattered in a gentle curve in the remote South Pacific region, people have survived unbelievable hardships and the challenges of isolation by dint of their strength. During struggles and heartache, the simple folk music of the panpipe was played to calm fears and raise spirits: a critical skill for a scattered population set between Papua New Guinea and Vanuatu. On two major parallel island chains, extending some 1,800 kilometres, the resilient and resourceful people of the Solomon Islands have long believed in the powerful physiological and emotional effects of music: using panpipes to enhance moods and human behaviour. Music is played on the birth of a child, to announce a marriage, mark a death and reflect the collective state of mind of the community. Enharmonic key changes and subtle tonal shifts are used to influence a state of mind while distinct musical pulses have a proven effect on heart rates. Slow rhythms – such as soothing lullabies – nurture relaxation by slowing the heart rate and aiding restfulness. In contrast, up-tempo beats heighten our

Photo: Kamal Azmi/DFAT

levels of excitement via peptides in the brain, energising muscles, stimulating adrenaline and elevating emotions. Music can tantalise every sensory switch by using the right pitch, correct pace and a well-chosen volley of notes. Using bamboo-carved panpipes, the rhapsodies of the Solomon Islands form an important part of the islanders' musical fabric by evoking pure emotions to boost mood, soothe fatigue, ease pain and create peace – a true melodic triumph.

Panpipes, as a multi-tubed instrument, require precise positioning of the mouth; steady the tubes against the chin before blowing across the rim of each tube to create a note. By practicing, you'll become familiar with the panpipe scale so that you can start picking out melodies to play. The pipes are tuned to a diatonic scale, though some varieties elsewhere in the world have three rows of pipes that enable a chromatic scale – like a piano, harp or guitar. In the Western world, some panpipes are concert tuned so that they can be played with other instruments.

Though it has a limited musical range, the panpipe is used much like any other instrument to signify heartbreak or heightened ardour in the form of creeping chords and rising scales. Urgent, dizzying use of the tongue can take a calm refrain (a gentle kiss) up to a breathless tempo (passion), or playing with wondrous delicacy can represent a tender embrace. To play the panpipes is a skill and an honour in the Solomon Islands and the most famous of the archipelago's panpipe group is the Narasirato Pan Pipe Band from Malaita Island. In their village in the virgin rainforest, the panpipers have no electricity and can only be reached by canoe, as they are a long, two-day hike from the nearest major settlement. Yet, since forming in 1990, they have performed in Canada, New Zealand, England, Taipei, Vanuatu, Malaysia, Bahrain and Australia. Their songs are inspired by their ancestors;

sharks; spirits and nature, and are haunting, infectious reflections of the *Are'are* culture. Playing an unusual mix of bamboo panpipes, including a huge blown bass, the group also adds rich island harmonies. It sounds amazing in an auditorium, though the group insists that this bliss-inducing music, with its peaceful acoustic melodies, sounds best when heard against a backdrop of rustling palms, powdery sands and the warm, turquoise waters of the South Pacific.

Each community on the Solomon Islands has its own authentic tunes and style of performance. On some islands the musicians are women, on others men. For authentic music with integrity, there is never a mix. The islands of Roviana, Isabel and Guadalcanal share similar musical rituals while the capital city Honiara uses panpipe music during a ceremony to awaken the spirit world. On Malaita, scores of traditional tunes have extremely culturally diverse roots across ethnic groups – each set of panpipes is different too. Made from bamboo, which has grown wildly over the island for as long as anyone can remember, most are resonating cylindrical tubes, carved carefully to ensure they are inversely proportional. Narrowing a tube will sound 'reedy', while creating a wide one will sound 'flutey' – the range is added to by increasing breath pressure and lip tension, or partially corking the end. The most advanced players in Malaita can play any scale in any key, and are masters of vibrato. Each community has its own traditional name for their particular style of panpipe. To the *Are'are* people, they are known as either '*aunimako*' or '*aurerepi*'. Each year the Solomon Islands showcase their unique and diverse panpipe styles at the Festival of Pacific Arts – always to a standing ovation.

Apart from helping to keep their culture alive, the music of the Masina Pan Pipers and Narasirato Pan Pipe Band has helped to teach people about the musicians' little-known homeland. As the home of around 550,000 people, Solomon Islanders are predominantly Melanesian (95 per cent) with smaller Polynesian, Micronesian, Chinese and European communities. Kinship and clan ties run deep, as does culture and tradition, with more than 60 distinct languages spoken across the archipelago. On many islands, a system of barter is more popular than monetary transactions and the simple style of daily life, which revolves around fishing and farming, can appear a long way from the 21st-century Western world.

Contacts:
Solomon Islands Tourist Board
visitsolomons.com.sb

Solomon Tour Company
travelsolomons.com

ADELAIDE, AUSTRALIA

Once considered a sleepy country town, well away from all the hubbub and noise of Australia's buzzier cities, Adelaide has undergone a rapid transformation that has finally acknowledged its musical heart. Amongst a thriving small-bar scene, a world-class art and music culture has been slowly, and shyly, developed in the shadows. It didn't yell about it. Or make a fuss. Adelaide isn't a creative big-mouth. No, it simply nurtured a stand-out music scene by supporting artists, musicians and the role live music played in the city. An incredible 950 live music gigs take place each month in over 150 venues in the city and outer suburbs. The venues aren't huge, but then nor is Adelaide, with a population of just a little over 1.3 million. Still, everyone who picks up a guitar or a synth there hopes to be the next Cold Chisel, Paul Kelly, Hilltop Hoods, Wolf & Cub or AC/DC.

Adelaide's musical buzz has given the city a lever to economic development by bringing new visitors to its vibrant bars, halls and gig spaces. It has also benefited from inward investment from entrepreneurs, artist management and promoters. The extraordinary upward trajectory in Adelaide's rock, pop, blues, jazz, orchestral and indie bands has led to formal recognition by the United Nations as a city of music. On awarding it UNESCO status, the UN praised the city for its 'wonderful range of musical culture'. As the home of classical favourites the Australian String Quartet and consummate choral ensemble the Adelaide Chamber Singers, the city also supports legions of unsigned rock bands who cut their teeth gigging the circuit. Adelaide is in auspicious company, joining a prestigious roll-call of nineteen cities across the world celebrated for their music cultures. Credit must go to the State Government for its decision to bring top UK festival booker and WOMADelaide co-founder Martin Elbourne to the city in 2012 as Thinker in Residence. His report, 'The Future of Music', strengthened the city as a music hub and encouraged collaboration between musicians and music businesses. Adelaide has listened and is nurturing a culture where musicians can meet mentors and network. Bureaucratic headaches and red tape that once stood in the way of staging live music are no more. Work is also underway to create more affordable regional touring circuits so that new, young bands can get started – with more than A$ 3 million set aside to make music happen. As a gig-goer it takes very little effort to be neck-deep in the music scene all week.

Photo: Nicholas Harrison

Adelaide's commitment to live music has secured it plenty of public funding to attract popular festivals, such as WOMADelaide – the Australian spin-off of WOMAD (World Of Music and Dance), which draws thousands of visitors each March and has other festival sites in Wiltshire (UK), Extremadura (Spain), Taranaki (New Zealand) and Santiago (Chile). WOMADelaide transforms the beautiful inner-city Botanic Park for a four-day celebration of music, art and dance from across the globe. Another big draw is the Adelaide Fringe, which presents an eclectic programme covering everything from cabaret to comedy and circus – 900 events staged in a range of quirky venues across the city. Adelaide's Guitar Festival is also working closely with other cities on the UNESCO musical list to develop exchange programmes – a recent project has been announced with flamenco guitarists in Seville for 2017.

UNESCO's other cities of music include the Beatles' hometown of Liverpool (UK), and Bogota (Colombia), a city which stages an ambitious calendar of free rock and pop mega-concerts for its citizens. It is fair to say that Adelaide is the lesser known musical city on UNESCO's list – though native Adelaidians point to their city's mix of stadiums and little hole-in-the-wall venues and insist recognition has been a long time coming. Flick through the local gig guide and you'll find a stack of live music on, whatever the day of the week, be it garage, blues, rock, punk, jazz, dance, classical or trance.

In the Adelaide Entertainment Centre, A-list international bands play to a capacity of around 12,000 people. Set on the corner of Port Road and Adam Street, the top-notch venue is served by train from the city centre as well as a free tram service. The Adelaide Festival Centre, a short walk from the Central Business District (CBD) plays host to musicals, opera, plays and festivals. The home of multiple spaces, including the Festival Theatre, Dunstan Playhouse, Space, Her Majesty's Theatre, the Amphitheatre and the Artspace Gallery, the Festival Centre is located on King William Street and easily reached by public transport.

As the largest venue by far in Adelaide, the Royal Adelaide Showground is used for big-budget extravagant gigs by major pop stars as well as big international music events. Close to the CBD on the south-west end of the Adelaide Parklands, the Showground connects to the city by bus, tram and train.

The Worlds End Hotel in Hindley Street is one of Adelaide's most popular live music venues, and stages live gigs every night of the week. Attracting a lively crowd of loyal devotees, Monday nights are open mic night, where new talent and acts can have a crack at the big time. Tuesdays and Wednesdays are reserved for acoustic groups and Thursdays are devoted to rock. Weekends are a mix of visiting DJs and support acts that rage all night until the wee small hours.

The HG Complex on North Terrace hosts live bands at least a couple of times a week. Set on three levels, this is a heck of a place to party. On Saturdays it is packed with dance music lovers who come for big-name DJs and light shows. As a polar opposite, the oh-so cosy Bull and Bear on King William Street is solely focused on promoting new talent. Expect to find an eclectic music mix on the bill throughout the week with Thursday nights devoted to hip-hop and R&B. On Fridays the Bull and Bear draws a devoted indie music crowd while Saturdays is all about new DJs and their turntables. As a city, Adelaide is also proving flexible in staging music in non-traditional venues such as the city's Central Market. It is now possible, for example, to have live gigs in all manner of corners of the city, from acoustic singer-songwriters to Adelaide's best reggae.

Adelaide, together with Canberra, was once one of the most often mocked Australian cities. Banal, decried the critics – yet as the capital of South Australia, Adelaide has historically been the hub of free-spirited and free-thinking people. It was the first place to abolish sexual and racial discrimination, to do away with capital punishment, to recognise Aboriginal land rights, to give women voting rights and legalise nude swimming. Today it can be proud of standing by the many guys with day jobs who play gigs for love and dreams, and inspiring those with a record deal – such as Sony-signed Adelaide producer M4sonic, the man responsible for the beats on hit song 'The Fox (What Does the Fox Say?)' – to spread the love to all the city's unsigned heroes.

Contacts:
WOMADelaide
womadelaide.com.au

Gig Guide Australia
gigguideaustralia.com.au

THE AMERICAS

DOLLYWOOD, TENNESSEE, USA

With her platinum blonde hair, petite but voluptuous figure and sparkling blue eyes, the over-sized voice, breathless vocals and southern country twang of Dolly Parton is instantly recognisable to music lovers all over the globe. Dolly famously grew up as one of twelve children in a one-room cabin in Tennessee with her parents Robert and Avie, both also from large families. Her most touching song – 'Coat of Many Colors' – recounts a tear-jerking true story from her impoverished childhood. With her husband, Carl Dean (who she met at a local laundromat), Dolly raised her five youngest siblings in Tennessee: a state inextricably linked with the Parton legacy and where she continues to reside and run her business interests today. A bronze sculpture of Dolly sits on the courthouse lawn in her hometown of Sevierville and she owned and ran radio stations WSEV 930 AM and WDLY 105.5FM there from 1991 until she sold them in 2000. Many of the songs she sings evoke the spirit and landscape of Tennessee and in 2004 Dolly recorded the song 'My Tennessee Hills' with folk icon Janis Ian for Ian's much-acclaimed album *Billie's Bones*.

In 1986 she was inducted into the Nashville Songwriters Hall of Fame and she was honoured with the Country Music Association's very first 'Country Music Honors' award in 1993 – the sole recipient of this honour. She was inducted to the Country Music Hall of Fame in 1999, has earned five BMI Million-Air Performance Awards and numerous BMI Songwriter Citations of Achievement. Since 2002 Dolly has been Tennessee's official ambassador for film and music and received the National Medal of Arts in 2005. Dolly has stars on both Nashville and Hollywood's Walks of Fame, and once entered a Dolly Parton look-alike contest and failed to win. Today Dolly is also the owner and namesake of Smoky Mountain area theme park, 'Dollywood', located in Pigeon Forge, Tennessee.

Though her augmented 48DD breasts are reportedly insured for around $1 million, it is the Dolly Parton voice

Photo: Brian Stansberry

Photo: Edward C. Denny

that has won her legions of fans across the genres of country, pop, folk and rock. There is only one Dolly Parton: an artist who can woo a 100,000-strong crowd in a muddy field at Glastonbury Festival, delight an audience of school children a fraction of the size, and turn a auditorium of politicians to mush. Best-selling records 'Jolene' and 'Here You Come Again' have seen Dolly rank high in VH1's Greatest Women of Rock 'N' Roll, while her iconic hit love song, 'I Will Always Love You', polled No. 1 in the 100 Greatest Love Songs of Country Music awards. 'Nine to Five' won Dolly an Oscar nomination (not bad for a song that came to her whilst Dolly tapped her perfectly-manicured finger nails on the set of the film of the same name ...) As one of the Top 40 Greatest Women in Country Music, Dolly's duet, 'Islands in the Stream', with fellow country singer Kenny Rogers, is still voted one of the CMT 100 Greatest Country Duets of All Time. Dolly regularly appears in the CMT list of the 20 Sexiest Women in Country Music and is a recipient of the Songwriters Hall of Fame's prestigious Johnny Mercer Award, the Cliffie Stone Pioneer Award from the Academy of Country Music, and was inducted into the American Songwriters Hall of Fame in 2001. In 2011 she received the Grammy Lifetime Achievement Award. Parton has a pinball machine in her honour (it plays her number one single 'Here You Come Again' and is a highly sought after piece of Dolly memorabilia) and is the godmother to Miley Cyrus. In poker, a hole card combination of a 9 and a 5 is called a 'Dolly Parton' after her song and movie. The world's first cloned mammal, Dolly the sheep, was named after Parton.

Dollywood is Tennessee's most popular visitor attraction with 40 rides, fifteen exceptional musical shows and restaurants that showcase Southern-style dining. As the host of five of the South's biggest festivals, Dollywood has become an award-winning destination that places a huge emphasis on ensuring every guest receives a warm, inviting 'Dolly Parton-style' smile from every member of staff at the entertainment park. Since it opened in 1986, Dollywood has grown to 150 acres following $110 million of expansion work and is now one of the Top 50 theme parks in the world. A mix of local history, culture, food and music has enabled Dolly to share her love of the Great Smoky Mountains and country music with millions of visitors each year. Guests can eat Tennessee-style barbecue ribs in Aunt Granny's restaurant, enjoy musical shows in the 450-seat Back Porch Theatre and ride the Smoky Mountain Rampage with Klondike Katie, a 110-ton coal-fired steam train built in 1943, still trundling the tracks through the rocky foothills today. The rides and shows are all liberally sprinkled with Dolly's own special brand of charm-rich fairy dust to ensure a heart-warming seasonal family day out that comes with its own 100-acre, 300-room resort, complete with story-telling spots, fire pits, swings and hammocks amidst gorgeous mountain scenery.

Dolly's amazing vocal talent was evident from a young age, and she was already recording on a small label and appearing at the Grand Ole Opry at the age of thirteen. Once she finished high school in Sevier County in 1964, Dolly headed to the bright lights of Nashville to launch her career as a country singer. After marrying Carl in 1966 (they recently celebrated their golden wedding anniversary) Dolly's singing caught the attention of Porter Wagoner, who hired her to appear on his TV show, and their duets soon became famous. By 1970, her immense popularity and fame overshadowed Porter's and Dolly launched as a solo artist in 1974. She was a natural for TV talk shows as a 5ft 0" beauty and lots of television work and movies followed. Today, Parton has a special place in the hearts and minds of the music-loving general public worldwide for her big-hearted charity work and strong Tennessee family roots. Today, she continues to record new material whilst running Dolly Parton Media Industries – a multi-billion business empire. 'I'm not offended by dumb blonde jokes,' she once claimed, 'because I know that I'm not dumb – and I also know I'm not blonde. There's a heart beneath the boobs and a brain beneath the wig.'

Despite the hardships of childhood poverty, Dolly was encouraged by her family to pursue her dreams, and she always felt inspired and curious about the world. A prolific writer (she penned 'Jolene' and 'I Will Always Love You' – later covered by Whitney Houston – in a single sitting one evening), she is particularly proud of the work she continues to do to increase literacy rates in Tennessee. She remains very much at the helm of the Dollywood Foundation, which funds the Dolly Parton Imagination Library and provides a book a month to children in communities across North America and the United Kingdom. Her drive to spearhead the campaign to get children reading is powered by the experiences of her own father who didn't get a chance to get an education because he needed to work in the fields. Not that her own upbringing has held her back – far from it, she is an astute business woman in control of her work. Unlike many of the world's most famous singer-songwriters, Dolly Parton owns all of the publishing rights to every song she's ever written and even famously denied Elvis the rights to record 'I Will Always Love You' because it meant she'd need to sign it over to Colonel Tom Parker, his manager.

Contacts:
Dollywood
dollywood.com

Dolly Parton
dollyparton.com

Tennessee Tourism
tnvacation.com

GRACELAND, TENNESSEE, USA

Few stars of the music world experienced a meteoric rise to fame like Elvis Aaron Presley. In the early 1950s, Elvis sang gospel songs for his local church. In 1955 he signed his first big recording deal with RCA records. By 1956 he was a household name America-wide. As a young boy, Elvis promised his parents he would put an end to their money worries. The family struggled to make ends meet but Elvis pledged that he would buy them the finest house in town one day. Few could have dreamt that this poor small-town boy would reach superstardom and change pop culture around the world forever.

As soon as he hit the big-time, Elvis fulfilled his promise and splashed out on a grand stately mansion for his family to live in. Called Graceland, this opulent home set on an expansive acreage was much more than a status symbol – it was a debt of gratitude to the parents, who had supported him through years of struggle. For everything it represented, Graceland was a special place of deep sentiment to Elvis that was close to his heart. Over the twenty years that he lived there, he shared the mansion with many friends and relatives and delighted in it as a source of pride and joy and the embodiment of the great American Dream. Today this

Photo: Nick Shields

grandiose colonial revival-style home is where legions of rock 'n' roll fans from every corner of the globe arrive to pay homage to a musical legend. For Elvis Presley fans it is the ultimate pilgrimage: an unforgettable journey into the private world of a man millions know simply as 'The King'.

Elvis paid $102,500 on 25 March 1957 for Graceland and its 13.8 acre plot. At 10,266 square feet the property was plenty big enough for his extended family. It had been built in 1939 by urologist professor Dr Thomas Moore and named after his wife's aunt Grace, who originally owned the land. The rich rolling verdant pasture around Graceland nourished herds of fine cattle and the Moores' cattle farm specialised in breeding Herefords. The Moores had already agreed to sell to the YMCA for $35,000 so Elvis made them an impossible-to-refuse offer. Once the sale was agreed, and a $1,000 down payment paid, Elvis's parents Vernon and Gladys and his grandma moved in (on 16 May 1957). Elvis was out of state filming his cinematic blockbuster *Jailhouse Rock*, but returned to spend his first night at Graceland on 26 June 1957. Today, after modification and expansion, Graceland is over 17,552 square feet in size – with its largest and most significant expansion since opening to the public slated for the summer of 2017. The 200,000-square foot $45 million 'Elvis: Past, Present & Future' entertainment complex will be five times the size of the current visitor centre. An interactive multi-media attraction, it will offer an immersive pop culture experience that promises to reveal previously unheard parts of the Elvis story in an unprecedented way – it is certain to be a hit with the fans.

Even without all the gadgetry, Graceland is no ordinary home, with five sets of stairs, several enormous fireplaces and a gorgeous kidney-shaped swimming pool. Elvis had the iconic music gates installed by John Dillars of Memphis Doors

Inc before anyone moved in and these immediately made a statement on Highway 51 South in Memphis, Tennessee. In 1991, Graceland claimed its place on the American National Register of Historic Places. Located just twelve miles south of downtown Memphis, the name of Highway 51 South was changed to Elvis Presley Boulevard in 1971. His parents added a chicken coop and a vegetable garden while Elvis set an old brick smokehouse as a pistol shooting range. The trophies, medals, cups and every possible award bestowed on Elvis chronicle an amazing career. You'll be dazzled by walls of gold records and beautiful rose gardens but also fascinated by concert posters, shirt buttons, shopping lists, receipts and lots more. Despite its grand, rock-star trappings, Graceland feels refreshingly homely. It is also an informative, enlightening and schmaltz-free place to tour, balancing respectful reflection on Elvis's vast musical legacy with an incredible level of visitor access. Every room provides a deeper insight into a man we all feel we know – the King of Rock 'n' Roll. More than 15 million people have walked Graceland's shag-pile carpets since it opened for tours in 1982. Some of his most devoted fans have paid more than a hundred visits a piece.

When Elvis Presley died in his home on 16 August 1977 after a racquetball game at 4am, we were all given a glimpse of his bizarre routine. Sports in the wee small hours wasn't an unusual pastime for Elvis. He would also call friends over to watch movies in the early hours, and booked dental appointments for midnight. Dinner could be anytime between 2am and 6am. At the time he died, Elvis had been reading a book in the bathroom. Former beauty queen Ginger Alden, his then girlfriend, called an ambulance after finding him unconscious on the floor. He was pronounced dead at the nearby Baptist Medical Center. At 4pm that day, Vernon Presley sombrely announced to the reporters gathered on the steps of Graceland: 'My son is dead.'

The whole world was shocked by the death of Elvis Presley at only 42 years of age. An estimated 80,000 fans made the pilgrimage to Graceland on the very first day to pay their respects to The King. Today, in the run-up to Christmas, the Graceland Experience celebrates what was Elvis's very favourite time of year. They do him proud: fans gather from all over world at the front gates of Graceland for the annual lighting of the Christmas decorations. It is an epic sight with the entire house illuminated by fairy-lights and lanterns with millions of tiny blue lights twinkling along the driveway. Throughout every room, trees are decorated with Presley family artefacts. Santa in his sleigh is the holiday season showpiece, accompanied by many favourite Elvis Christmas songs. Christmas tickets for Graceland have been snapped up in minutes every year since Elvis's ex-wife Priscilla opened the estate to the public for tours. His only child, Lisa Marie Presley, inherited Graceland when she turned 25 in 1993 and continues to operate it today: a memorial to her father, a snake-hipped unknown who made musical history on 5 July 1954, when he recorded 'That's All Right (Mama)' at Memphis-based Sun Studio – and changed the course of music forever. More than a dozen No.1 singles and 31 movie roles helped Elvis claim his place as one of the most iconic entertainers of the 20th century. Look out for special key dates in the Elvis calendar, as well as the incredible celebrations during Elvis Week, in August, when Graceland stages a wide variety of different memorial and celebratory, shows and concerts.

Contacts:
Graceland tours
graceland.com

Elvis Presley
elvis.com

Memphis Tourist Office
memphistravel.com

NEW ORLEANS, LOUISIANA, USA

New Orleans positively buzzes with excitement as news spreads of the carnival floats leaving the 'den' – a colloquial term for the cavern-like warehouse where Mardi Gras paraphernalia is built and stored throughout the year. Mardi Gras has been celebrated in cities worldwide since 1699 but for many Americans, New Orleans IS Mardi Gras – no one does it better. Culminating with oh-so hedonistic Fat Tuesday in February, this traditional season of carnival merriment heralds the penitential season of Lent with Cajun feasting, pumping jazz music, garish outfits and dance. Dozens of lively parades provide a colourful prelude to Mardi Gras day, so whether you are on St. Charles Avenue with the family, catching glittery beads from a Central Business District balcony or enjoying the hand-sewn intricate costumes on Canal before a night of partying in the French Quarter, be prepared to scream … 'Throw me something, Mister!' really loud in order to fill a bag full of inexpensive trinkets tossed from each outlandish, multi-coloured passing float.

   In the middle of the carnival chaos, music can be heard in New Orleans at every turn: from the sound-systems on the slow-moving floats and the music blasting out of sidewalk bars, to the high-register brass tones of the

trumpet. A sign on a time-faded wall in a popular New Orleans club says: 'The trumpet is an instrument created to appease the gods; a musical device that takes a month to learn and a lifetime to master.' Certainly, the defining quality of the trumpet is the crisp clarity that can be achieved from the instrument's cup-shaped mouthpiece, slides, valves and gleaming brass body. In New Orleans, the trumpeter is the musical king who can turn simple, buzzing vibrations into unique peeling tones using air blown through pursed lips into a mouthpiece. Clever manipulation of the wave vibrations as they travel inside the trumpet is achieved by pressing and releasing valves (keys). True trumpeting royalty can achieve an incredible range and rally of notes by lengthening the distance the sound must travel before it exits the bell. Rapid fingering of the keys, combined with a variety of lip movements, actively controls the quality and pitch of the sound – as does tongue movement and moisture from the breath. The trumpet is a true challenge to master, requiring considerable skill and time to practice.

In New Orleans the trumpet has always been the 'lead' instrument in the traditional jazz of the city, carrying the melody of most tunes because it is loud enough to be heard above everything else – regardless of what the other front line instruments are doing. Historically, many New Orleans jazz trumpeters fell into three categories – those that could read music, those that could follow a written chord progression and those that could play by ear (known as 'faking it' in club-land). Today, despite several periods in history when jazz trumpeting went in and out of fashion, it seems unimaginable that the musical scene in New Orleans could ever survive without its world-class trumpeters. There are dozens of note – some living legends and some up-and-coming artists – but many are following in the footsteps of the one-and-only Louis 'Satchmo' Armstrong – the greatest trumpeter in the Big Easy's authentic jazz experience. Others emulate the much-respected Lionel Ferbos, who played with everyone from Fats Pichon to Harold Dejan and had a regular monthly gig at the Palm Court Jazz Café in the French Quarter well past the age of 100.

Irvin Mayfield has become a well-known name in New Orleans since recording in his own small groups as well as with big-name percussionist Bill Summers. Try and catch him playing in the JW Marriot Hotel and at his name sake club inside the Royal Sonesta on Bourbon Street – he is part of the city's establishment now but was once one of the scene's youngsters. Another icon of the trumpeting world is Kermit Ruffins, whose performances and recordings almost define the New Orleans spirit. Expect renditions of everything from Louis Armstrong and Sly Stone to Amy Winehouse at his regular gigs throughout the Big Easy. Jeremy Davenport is another exciting talent on the New Orleans jazz circuit, playing with Harry Connick Jr. before taking a long-standing weekend residency at the Ritz-Carlton New Orleans. His contemporary Shamarr Allen is renowned for his bold, brash style and versatility – he has played for both Willie Nelson and for Barack Obama, during his presidency. Another great jazzman is Terence Blanchard: a player of true quality that many in New Orleans hail the top trumpeter and jazz player in the world. At the other end of the celebratory roll-call is Leroy James and Wendell Brunious – still both relatively unsung and underrated but with the skills and class to excite any bandstand they frequent. A trumpeting star who is rising fast, Mark Braud, has grown to become an integral part of the New Orleans jazz scene – he has worked with the Preservation Hall Jazz Band and frequently plays in many of the clubs and venues around the French Quarter, including the Palm Court Jazz Café.

During the madcap revelry of colourful Mardi Gras celebrations, many of the best-loved songs refer to the importance of the trumpet and the role it plays in New Orleans culture. One of the favourites is a bouncy 1950s tune made famous by The Hawkettes, entitled 'Mardi Gras Mambo'. With its gritty feel and Creole-style chord progression, the tune encapsulates the musical spirit of the city, especially in the following lyrics: 'Down in New Orleans where the blues was born, it takes a cool cat to blow a horn.' It certainly does – and the legacy that Louis Armstrong has left his music-loving hometown, as trumpeter, singer and bandleader, has ensured it remains a compelling destination, steeped in jazz history and musical lore. Legends still play homage to the man who traded a career as a labourer to concentrate on playing trumpet at honky-tonk gigs full-time. Every jazz venue in New Orleans has a story about Louis Armstrong, including his first star-struck encounters with jazz legends Bix Beiderbecke and Jack Teagarden; his four troubled marriages and why in 1926 he switched to the trumpet from the cornet.

Contact:
Mardi Gras New Orleans
mardigrasneworleans.com

New Orleans Tourism
neworleanscvb.com

Louisiana Tourism
louisianatravel.com

OHIO, USA

Opera pilgrims keen to retrace the size XXL steps of Luciano Pavarotti generally book a ticket to the river-valley town of Modena in northern Italy where 'The Big P' (as he was known with great affection) was laid to rest in his family tomb in September 2007. Yet a much more congenial shrine is a simple neighbourhood food joint in Ohio owned by Pavarotti's old friend Gina Ciresi. The Zeppe chain is a string of three dozen franchise pizza bars that serve up no-fuss Italian fare US-wide. Ciresi, a former opera singer herself, trained with Pavarotti in Genoa in 1956 under Paolo Campogalliani as well as at the Italian Opera Centre in Milan. Today, as a tribute to her famous friend, Ciresi throws open her Pavarotti-themed restaurant to fans from as far away as Jacksonville (Florida), Jakarta (Indonesia) and Johannesburg (South Africa).

Managed by her son Joseph Ciresi, the restaurant is a gallery of dozens of pictures, posters and oil paintings of Luciano Pavarotti, honouring one of Italy's greatest voices. Fittingly for a tenor who adored his food, Zeppe's also serves a Pavarotti calzone that is stuffed with his favourite pasta, spaghetti.

Pavarotti and Ciresi were study buddies – she was by his side when he got his big break and heard that he had been chosen to sing at the New York Metropolitan Opera in 1963. After pursuing a singing career in Italy, Ciresi retired in 1975 to marry American-based businessman John Ciresi and have a family. She remained friends with Pavarotti, reuniting with him many times over the years, and becoming a key fundraising member for the Pavarotti International Voice Competition. He dined at the restaurant in Darrow Road, Hudson several times over the years and he was always

Photo: AP Wirephoto

welcomed with great gusto. An abiding memory of the locals is a night when Pavarotti drove for over an hour from a concert to claim his favourite table at Zeppe's. His meal of choice? An extra-large calzone (folded and stuffed pizza) filled with Ciresi's cream-covered pasta. Today, Pavarotti fans seated at the very same table can expect to be regaled with star-studded stories as they mop up their sauce with hunks of fresh Italian bread. The Pavarotti vibe is upped even more on special calendar days, such as his birthday, or the date of his death at 71, when tribute acts provide entertainment and Ciresi herself performs.

Pavarotti has long garnered warm support from his friends and fans. Even his funeral ceremony had a party atmosphere with a host of international celebrities jetting in to pay their respects together with more than 50,000 'ordinary' music lovers from every corner of the globe. As the self-proclaimed 'King of the High Cs' – in 1966 he became the first opera tenor to hit all nine 'high Cs' with his full voice in the aria '*Quel destin*' in '*La Fille du Regiment*' – Pavarotti's honey-sweet ringing tone set a standard for operatic tenors of the post-war era. He remains the most commercially successful tenor of our time; extending his presence far beyond the opera scene. His pop collaborations, and childlike charm and charisma, matched his generous frame and brought him millions of TV fans across the world, many of whom had only a glancing familiarity with serious opera. His huge audience – drawn across numerous countries, various social classes and every age – proved that Pavarotti was so much more than the great male operatic voice of his generation. The 1970s are often hailed as his glory years and it was certainly the decade during which Pavarotti's remarkable voice first grabbed world attention. It has been said that Pavarotti's supreme confidence and natural ability to find the heart of a character compensated for his lack of intellectual presence and ability to study music to the nth degree. Though his ego was substantial, Pavarotti had a rather simple happy-go-lucky style, clearly revelling in the slavish adoration that operatic superstardom brought him and willingly appearing on talk shows and daytime TV. His voice was powerful, penetrating and possessed brilliant clarity with a clear Italian diction and manipulative use of musicality and lyrics, lauded as absolute perfection.

In the 1980s Pavarotti amplified this fame as part of the Three Tenors projects, in which he shared the stage with Plácido Domingo and José Carreras, first in concerts associated with the World Cup and later in world tours. The Three Tenors phenomenon sold millions of recordings and videos and led to the Pavarotti and Friends charity concerts of the 1990s with rock stars such as Elton John, Bono and Sting. Sell-out stadium concerts and franchise broadcasts propelled him to the role of Operatic Titan until he began a Grand Farewell World Tour in 2004, due to poor health and mobility problems. Physical ailments caused several performances to be cancelled yet at the end of a string of 'Tosca' performances at The Met on 13 March 2004, the audience erupted into thunderous applause. Pavarotti looked genuinely humbled by the fifteen-minute standing ovation and ten curtain calls that night in what was the culmination of 379 performances at The Met, of which 357 were in fully staged operatic productions.

Yet while Luciano Pavarotti adored the glitz, wealth and glamour of his fame, he came from very modest beginnings. Born to a baker father (who was an amateur tenor himself) and a factory worker mother in 1935, he listened to opera recordings as a child and watched the movies of Mario Lanza, whose image he professed to imitating. After finishing school he took a student teacher job for two years before deciding to fulfil his dream of becoming a singer. Pavarotti got his big breakthrough aged 26 when he won a competition at the Teatro Reggio Emilia. Later that same year he made his debut as Rodolfo in Puccini's *'La Bohème'* with an international career beckoning just two years later. His Covent Garden debut in 1963 helped him become a darling of the British opera scene and he went on to take the part of Idamante in Mozart's 'Idomeneo' at the Glyndebourne Festival the same year. Other major milestones in Pavarotti's career came in 1965 when he joined the Sutherland-Williamson company on an Australian tour to sing Edgardo to Ms Sutherland's Lucia. He made his first appearances at La Scala in Milan and at the Metropolitan Opera a year later, singing with Mirella Freni, a childhood friend, in *'La Bohème'*.

Over the years Pavarotti increasingly became a regular target of newspaper gossip columnists. In 1997, he left his wife of more than 30 years Adua, to live with his 26-year-old assistant, Nicoletta Mantovani. His appetite for life and love was as big as his personality – and his waistband. Critics of Pavarotti ensured his weight gains became a topic of public discussion. They also slated him for a propensity to pull out of sell-out concerts at the 11th hour. As you'd expect, Gina Ciresi defends against stories that threaten to blemish the memory of her friend as she talks diners through the photos that line Zeppe's walls. Keen to dine at one of Pavarotti's favourite food joints? No need to book a table and your visit can be combined with a tour of the Rock & Roll Hall of Fame in Cleveland, a 60-minute drive away (*see*: Cleveland).

Contacts:
Zeppe's Restaurant
zeppes.com

Cleveland Tourism
thisiscleveland.com

Pavarotti
lucianopavarotti.com

DEATH VALLEY NATIONAL PARK, CALIFORNIA, USA

The image is striking: a lone gnarled Joshua tree standing twisted in the desert. The music is everywhere: utterly inescapable during the late 1980s when *The Joshua Tree* sold more than 25 million copies worldwide. The band is U2: four guys from Ireland who combined an original sound with honest lyrics and a challenging social message to build up a fanatical following of fans around the world. It was *The Joshua Tree* that propelled them into international superstardom and the supporting tour that became a mammoth success story, spawning the documentary *Rattle and Hum*. Since the release of *The Joshua Tree*, the success of U2 has been epic, with *Achtung Baby, Pop, How to Dismantle an Atomic Bomb* and the critically acclaimed *All That You Can't Leave Behind*. In 2005, U2 were inducted into the Rock & Roll Hall of Fame. *Songs of Innocence*, released in September 2014, broke the mould as a free download for its first month and a half. U2 has also released a number of fine compilations, sold more than 145 million albums and won numerous MTV, Brit, Q, Billboard, Grammy, Golden Globe and American Music Awards. *The Joshua Tree* alone topped the charts in over twenty countries, selling well over 25 million copies, and winning Grammy Awards for 'Album of the Year' and 'Best Rock Performance'. In 2007, the band's 20th anniversary, it was *The Joshua Tree* U2 chose to release as a remastered edition in commemoration. In 2014, the album was deemed 'culturally, historically, or aesthetically significant' by the US Library of Congress and selected for preservation on the National Recording Registry: the musical vaults of our generation.

Originally a five-piece known as 'Feedback', they were formed by drummer Larry Mullen (born 31 October 1961) and included Adam Clayton (born 13 March 1960) on bass, Paul Hewson (later nicknamed 'Bono Vox' and eventually just 'Bono', born 10 May 1960) on vocals and Dave Evans (later nicknamed 'The Edge', born 8 August 1961) on guitar. Dave's brother, Dick, also played guitar for a while, but left Feedback very early on to join another Dublin band, the Virgin Prunes. Feedback quickly changed their name to 'The Hype,' and began rehearsing on weekends and after school as often as possible, forming genuine friendships and developing an undeniable musical chemistry. The band's big break came at a talent show in Limerick, Ireland, in March 1978 when U2 was born (yes, they'd changed their name – again). They won and, with CBS Records' Jackie Hayden as a judge, U2 won a £500 cash prize and studio time to record their first demo.

Though the band had been together just eighteen months, they convinced Dublin businessman Paul McGuinness to manage them. They became a big name on the local gig scene and nurtured a loyal fan base. In September 1979, U2 released its first single, an Irish-only release called 'U2:3' which topped the national charts. The band struggled to attract any attention for a while outside Ireland until they were signed up by Island Records to their first international contract in March 1980. When the album *Boy* was released in October of that year it earned rave reviews in both the Irish and UK press. U2's first tour in Europe and the USA raised the band's profile further. Their second album, 1981's *October* did much to prove that rock bands don't need to shed their personal beliefs to court popular success. The 1983 release of *War*, U2's third album, brought even greater international fame with the album's first single, 'New Year's Day,' their first legitimate hit single, reaching the number ten spot on the UK charts and almost cracking the Top 50 in the US. It was hard to find a time of the day that MTV wasn't playing the song's video. Tour dates sold out as MTV's heavy airplay cemented U2's reputation as a top-notch live act. The release of 1984's *The Unforgettable Fire* saw the band expanding its tour itinerary to more countries than ever before. *Rolling Stone* magazine named them its 'Band of the 80s' as Bono and the boys learned to deal with the glare of international stardom. Using their superstar profile for charitable purposes soon became part of the character of the band. First, the Live Aid concert for Ethiopian famine relief in July 1985 – an epic musical fundraiser watched by more than a billion people worldwide at which the foursome stole the show. At the 1986 'Conspiracy of Hope' tour for Amnesty International, U2 helped sell out arenas and stadiums. Amnesty International tripled its membership in the process and the band earned tremendous respect.

Yet, for fans over the world, it was the band's fifth studio album in 1987 that marked its musical peak. For many reasons, *The Joshua Tree* had a lyrical ease about it – U2 were comfortable with the tag 'rock band with a conscience' and relaxed about the meaning and passion they brought to their music. Having spent an increased amount of time in the USA, the band been troubled by their contradictory

Photo: Arjun R

feelings about America and felt that they needed to address them. In *The Joshua Tree*, Bono questioned faith, social injustices, governmental oppression, terrorism and drug addiction, and suggested that parts of America weren't just geographical and geological deserts but morally and spiritually arid too.

The album debuted at number one in the UK and achieved equal success in the US. *The Joshua Tree* tour sold out stadiums around the world as U2 accepted the mantle of one of the biggest bands on the planet. 'With or Without You' and 'I Still Haven't Found What I'm Looking For' gave U2 their first number one singles in the US and even *TIME* magazine put U2 on its cover as print media, broadcasters and documentary makers clambered to pay tribute to the band in words, music and pictures. The picture of the single twisted Joshua tree on the back of the album cover has become one of the most iconic rock music images of all time. It conveyed a thousand words. It drove home a sense of geography. It echoed the band's fascination for American landscapes and the metaphors they represented. According to U2's art director Anton Corbijn, one of the titles originally tossed around for the album was 'The Desert Songs'. The shoot site chosen for the artwork was California's Mojave Desert. As a hardy monocot native to the Mojave, the Joshua tree is a yucca palm and is one of the few plants that can survive the desert's relentlessly harsh climate. Mormon settlers gave the palm its name as they journeyed through the hot winds and dry sands. They believed its twisted branches resembled the biblical Joshua reaching up, hands pointed, to the sky in prayer. Bono, in particular, was struck by the physical and spiritual character of the palm, which he discovered had grown for two centuries or more – and so the new album was named.

The site of the Joshua tree can be accessed via California State Route 190 (the highway that bisects Death Valley National Park from west to east) about 21 kilometres (13 miles) southeast of the village of Keeler by the park's west gate. Joshua trees usually grow in groves, so the lone iconic tree that graced the back of the album cover has been relatively easy to pinpoint over the years. Certainly, it is a regular pilgrimage spot for U2 fans from around the world – especially Ireland – who decorate the base of the trunk with trinkets, scrawled messages and peace sculptures made from assembled rocks. In 2000, the tree was felled by strong desert winds. It is still lying on the sandy scrub, partially reshaped by the weather. A plaque reads: 'Have You Found What You're Looking For?' Another Joshua tree has grown a few metres away where there is a capsule, called the U2ube, where notes can be left for the legions of fans that arrive here to celebrate notable band anniversaries, birthdays and re-releases.

Heading to the Joshua Tree National Park in order to pay homage? You're in the wrong place: a four-hour drive south of U2's Joshua tree – a common mistake that results in an eight-hour wasted round-trip.

Contacts:
California Tourism
visitcalifornia.com

U2
u2.com

MIAMI, FLORIDA, USA

The beaches may form the heart of Miami but music is undeniably its soul. Few cities on the planet have as much music coursing through their veins. An irrepressible rhythmic pulse permeates this sassy, salsa city where every artery throbs with a percussive Latin beat. Little Havana's curbside *café con leche* bars are full of rapturous salsa melodies by breakfast time. While on the sultry sands of South Beach, sunworshippers enjoy staccato merengue rhythms with lunch. Samba and rumba classics ooze from open-top Corvettes as they glide along Ocean Drive. Strolling mariachi virtuosos serenade sombrero-clad bossa-nova kings. Every mall and diner resonates with music – and this intoxicating cocktail of Hispanic harmonies in this vibrant pan-Latino melting pot is so sweet you can almost imbibe it.

Miami's hybrid of Latin America cultures ensures it's a colourful, energetic city where a kaleidoscope of musical and linguistic styles intermingle to dramatic effect. Intense Nicaraguan dialects fuse with rich Puerto Rican drawls amidst a syncopated 'ta-tum-ta-tum' crossbreed of Cuban and Colombian salsa. In Spanish, salsa means sauce and Miami serves it *muy picante*, at a fiery, up-tempo pace. The musical nucleus of Miami is Calle Ocho. Hoisted national flags reflect the origins of this proud Hispanic community where Venezuelan *empanadas* (meat filled turnovers), Panamanian *patacones* (fried plantain), Cuban *frijoles negros* (black beans) and mouth-watering *tamales* (banana-leaf wrapped maize) from Peru are staple fare. More than 1 million tourists descend on Miami for Calle Ocho's annual street festival, a riot of colour that dominates the stretch between 27th and 4th Avenue. Thousands of hip-swaying *salseros* form a mile-long conga that snakes through sizzling *arepa* stalls to the drumming timbales. Mournful ballads derived from the idioms of Cuban farmers mix *claves*, *tumbao*, *cuica* and *cavaquinho* with tuneful laments. Visitors that can't make it to the March festival can get a taster every Sunday by arriving in Calle Ocho about lunchtime for an 'impromptu' weekly musical extravaganza. Veteran Latin musicians share the stage with aspiring chart-toppers as Little Havana's signature street becomes a carnival – simply follow the hubbub or ask directions from the elderly émigrés playing dominoes in the street.

Art and music keep easy company in Miami: a city daubed with bold, vibrant splashes of colour, from the turquoise sea and candy-pastel Art Deco buildings to glossy emerald palms, silvery sands and vibrant Latino cultures. The city's exciting artistic hub draws on the youthful energy of Miami that is the envy of many of North America's more sophisticated musical centres. Miami oozes sassy effervescence, welcoming a tsunami of singers, DJs, Latin-fusion bands and salsa-jazz musicians to a place that is famous for its frivolous fun so hot that it positively sizzles. Glittering rooftop parties attract a surfeit of record studio bosses, would-be hip-hop stars and far too many celebrities to count. Here, amongst the neon-lit bars and trendy all-night cafés, an interesting mix of penniless musicians and trendsetters with deep pockets from all over the globe party together. Business cards are swapped between shots of iced Don Julio tequila as demo tapes are exchanged and pitches made. Beautiful people draped over champagne buckets add glossy glamour to the shabby-chic music bars that have become the microcosm of cool. After trays of kaleidoscopic cocktails have been passed round, and the syncopated feel-good Latino rhythms turned

Photo: Gzz

up loud, it is time for Miami's emerging relative unknowns to showcase their work. Sometimes it is a heart-pounding cat-and-mouse chase to sign the new band. Other times, the punch-packing doesn't happen despite a dizzying array of show-stopping acts. Solo deals are signed amongst inflatable sculptures, soaring plastic palm trees and taxidermy sheep, and hit Miami's musical grapevine within a few hours.

Here the art, music and fashion worlds intertwine and the circuit of boutiques, fashion shows and flashing paparazzi bulbs herald the arrival of a rapper, catwalk model, actor, designer, salsa diva and toxic art critic – all ready to swap gossip and tips. Everyone is fascinated by the graffiti-music scene amongst the alternative artists of the ultra-funky Design District, Midtown and Wynwood. Small studios are home to singer-songwriters, DJs and session bands as well as the urban artists with marker pens and spray cans that are powering a metamorphosis in that part of the city. While contracts are signed for obscene amounts of cash in South Beach, this area records and creates on shoestring budgets. Anyone can scout the block and observe the musicians and artists at work – and many of the A-list do so in the hope of fan faring a rising star. There are often photography shoots by the former Versace mansion, always the site of a media scrum when Mark Anthony or P Diddy pose for a camera. For a captivating glimpse into the upper echelons of Miami musical celebrity look out for Lauryn Hill, Timbaland, Jay-Z, Beyoncé, Fat Joe, Usher and, of course, Gloria Estefan. Artists from America's East Coast like to collaborate with Miami-based artists, producers and studios as the ambiance in the clubs, on the beach and around the streets is something special. DJs drop new tracks every night in the clubs, starting new hip-hop trends, and the dance scene is a breeding ground for many of the USA's biggest hits.

Nowhere else can equal Miami for its heady mix of pulsating rhythms: a banging, beating, musical hotbed, with the city's diverse cultural population blending it up.

Contacts:
Miami Tourism
miamiandbeaches.com

LOS ANGELES, CALIFORNIA, USA

It was a defining moment for gangsta rap in 1996 when a high-profile member of hip-hop royalty was gunned down in the street. Rapper, actor and producer Tupac Shakur was only 25 when he died after the drive-by shooting. At the time, the US media slammed the genre for 'the grotesque violence that fills its art'. The 25-year-old was shot six times by a 40-calibre Glock handgun from a white Cadillac as he sat in his BMW in Las Vegas after watching a Mike Tyson fight. He was taken to hospital where his friends were so concerned for his safety that they arranged an armed guard to protect him, 24/7. After news that his condition had shown signs of improvement, fans were devastated to learn that Tupac had died after 'taking a turn for the worse'. Conspiracy theories abound, some intriguing and others utterly bizarre.

It was a shocking headline-grabbing death of a hip-hop star at the height of his career. Since then Tupac has become more and more of a myth-like figure as his murder has never been solved. Thousands of internet sites and message boards are dedicated to the mysteries and conspiracy theories surrounding his death on 13 September. He's not only a lodestar of hip-hop, but a global cultural phenomenon, and he was even resurrected to perform in CGI form with Snoop Dogg and Dr Dre in 2012. Since his death, the violence that helped establish Shakur's legacy has gradually become less a part of his story, especially in the USA. After being vilified by lawmakers during his life, Shakur's modern-day presence is much more mainstream. His poetry has been chosen for a Powerade TV advert and his music used in the Vatican's social media campaign – a strange career progression for a guy who served jail time for rape.

Today the enigmatic rapper is immortalised as a part of pop culture forever, even though he would now be a middle-aged man. More albums have been released after his death than were during his short-lived career, and he has sold millions of records. Yet despite the passage of time, there appears to be a fresh lead or theory on his homicide every few weeks.

While in jail in 1995, Shakur read a book by Italian philosopher Niccolò Machiavelli about the art of faking one's own death. Many fans have taken this as a sign that he has done the same and is still alive and well. Tupac fanatics have also scoured through his back catalogue and posthumous albums searching for lyrics predicting his death or hinting at his resurrection. Some have picked up subliminal messages and secret truths and are convinced that lyrics in 'Ain't Hard 2 Find' (1996 album *All Eyez on Me*) point to his resurrection: 'I heard a rumour I died, murdered in cold blood dramatized, Pictures of me in my final stage you know Mama cried, But that was fiction, some coward got the story twisted, Like I no longer existed, mysteriously missing'.

Other theorists cite the significance to the number seven in his life. Seven is a highly spiritual number in many religious texts including the Torah and some fans claim this has given him a Christ-like quality. For example, Tupac supposedly died at 4:03pm – a simple addition of the three numbers that make up the time give the equation: $4+0+3=7$. He was also shot on 7 September (dying several days later), a numerical cue that is seen as a holy sign that he will rise again. His death fell exactly seven months after the release of his final album *All Eyez on Me*. His career lasted seven years, which has again been seen as a divine representation of his time on earth. He has supposedly been spotted in a holiday resort in New Zealand and is also said to be living in Cuba. Many believe he is part of a witness protection programme by the FBI, living secretly in the US.

Today rap fans can visit the Los Angeles neighbourhoods in which Tupac grew up and built up his hip-hop label with a specialist tour company in California. Led by local guide Hodari, the tour journeys around Crenshaw Blvd, Baldwin Hills, Watts Towers and Compton, in a big, unmarked, armour-plated SUV. Hodari is a super-relaxed dude who is determined to provide a compelling, insightful and authentic experience, not a hyped-up OTT Hollywood star tour – so it feels just like you're cruising around the hood with a friend. It is fascinating to see LA from a native's perspective, warts and all, and to see the landmarks, faces and places that Shakur fed into his lyrics.

Tupac had famous conflicts with other rappers, producers and record-label staff members, including violent spats with The Notorious B.I.G. and the label Bad Boy Records, and speculation continues to surround the circumstances of his murder. David Myers, a retired police officer, claims he was paid to help Tupac fake his own death, hinting that he may still be alive. He made the claim while in a critical condition in hospital, saying he was paid $1.5 million to do it. Myers says he now wants the world to know the truth, and that he is now

Photo: danielle

ashamed of what he did. He said over 30 people were part of the cover-up, all paid by Tupac, including police, medics and various witnesses. Myers even claims a $50,000 'body double' was taken to the morgue. But the most outlandish theory is that aliens from the planet YILAMHAR used their extra-terrestrial powers to abduct Shakur. Apparently, the aliens have arranged for him to be surrounded by the 'phattest of honeys' and have promised to return him to earth after 100 years, after which he will have everlasting life. Even the cremation of Tupac's body has stirred up controversy, as rapper Surge Knight claimed he paid over $3 million to a man to personally cremate Shakur, only for the guy to do a runner with the cash (never to be seen again). Rap band The Outlawz have also claimed to have smoked the ashes of their mentor and friend. Other headlines place P Diddy at the scene of the crime.

Shortly after Shakur's death a Richie Rich track was released featuring these vocals by the dead rapper: 'I've been shot and murdered, can't tell you how it happened word for word but best believe that n*****' gonna get what they deserve.' Fans also claimed that documentary-makers were trying to cover up his death when full-length film *Resurrection* hit the screens – it was narrated by Tupac himself (there is no mistaking the swagger in his voice) though producers swear it was created via clever use of existing audio. He managed to scale the wall that stands tall between America's marginalised underclass to super-stardom – they state – meaning Tupac is astute enough to play the death card having made a heck of a lot of cash. His biggest hit – 'California Love' – featured a guest appearance by famed rapper-producer Dr. Dre. Today sales tally more than 75 million from Tupac albums worldwide.

Contacts:
LA Hood Life Tours
Tel: +1 (310) 722-3737

Discover Los Angeles
discoverlosangeles.com

LA City Tours
lacitytours.com

CLEVELAND, OHIO, USA

Cleveland, Ohio seems a strange place to have the Rock & Roll Hall of Fame. For a start it feels a long way from the pop parties, blues bars and hedonistic hell-raising hangouts of the rock 'n' roll world. It is also not somewhere you're like to find yourself passing through, unless you are road-tripping cross-country from America's east to west coast. Why, then, was it built in Cleveland? Well the original plan was for it to be housed in a New York brownstone until a group of Ohioans lobbied for Cleveland, citing the city's major music milestones. They argued that as Cleveland disc jockey Alan Freed popularised the term 'rock 'n' roll' on his integrated radio show and organised the country's first official rock 'n' roll concert, Cleveland was the natural host of the Rock & Roll Hall of Fame. Cleveland's citizens backed the bid in an overwhelming groundswell of public support. City officials then threw $65 million into the ring – a persuasive pitch: the Rock & Roll Hall of Fame was born. More than 10 million visitors, each with their own favourites and memories, have

Photo: Erik Drost

visited the Rock Hall in Cleveland since it opened in 1995. This is definitely one to add to the bucket list if you are an out-and-out music fan.

The brainchild behind the RARHOF was Atlantic Records founder and chairman Ahmet Ertegün, who understood the lure of rock star fanaticism and the tourism potential of an archive of the best-known and most influential artists, producers, engineers and other notable figures in the development of rock 'n' roll. Sure it's about the music, but fans so often want to get under the skin of their icons. He started gathering memorabilia that summed up the musical and cultural phenomenon of popular music, piecing together more than 50 visually exciting exhibits from the greatest stories and biggest names in rock 'n' roll. It is an epic project, on a monster scale: with four theatres, multiple interactive stations and seven floors of exhibits that contain weird and wonderful artefacts that tell the stories of everyone that helped create and perpetuate the craziest medium in the world, rock 'n' roll music. Nostalgic narratives remind us that rock 'n' roll used to scare parents; pop has inflamed preachers and disco lyrics have been so controversial that they've been banned by radio and TV stations all over the world. The largest collection of rock artefacts includes so many fascinating items, from Janis Joplin's psychedelic Porsche, upside-down cars from U2's 'Zoo TV' tour, Michael Jackson's sparkly glove, dozens of rock-god guitars, lots of typed contracts (check out the percentage charged by the agents, wow!), the scribbled lyrics of ideas that morphed into a zillion chart classics, dresses owned by Beyoncé, Johnny Cash's glitzed-up tuxedo and an outfit worn by Taylor Swift. Add this to all manner of memorabilia from Aerosmith, Bill Haley, Muddy Waters, Cream, Deep Purple, Miles Davis, ELO, Fleetwood

Mac, The Four Tops, Neil Diamond, Frank Zappa, Gladys Knight & The Pips and the Grateful Dead. There are set lists from Hall & Oates and ticket stubs, programmes and press cuttings from the likes of Metallica, Rod Stewart, The Hollies, Tina Turner, Isaac Hayes, Jimmy Cliff, Joan Jett, The Kinks, Led Zeppelin, Lynyrd Skynrd and Madonna. By the time you leave, you'll know all the tips and tricks of Martha and the Vandellas, Marvin Gaye, Buddy Guy and Frank Zappa. You'll have a whole new musical respect for Yes, ZZ Top and Nile Rogers; understand more about Pearl Jam and Nirvana; have been reminded how great The Pretenders were and have tracks by artists as diverse in style as The Beach Boys, Public Enemy, Quincy Jones, Ray Charles, The Sex Pistols, The Rolling Stones, Sly & the Family Stone; and be more familiar with the lyrics of the Velvet Underground, Tom Waits and Talking Heads. Favourite exhibits include a fragment of Otis Redding's crashed aeroplane, Joey Ramone's leather jacket, Paul Simonon's broken bass from the cover of *London Calling*, Jim Morrison's Boy Scouts shirt, Jimi Hendrix's childhood artwork, John Lennon's hand-written lyrics for 'Lucy in the Sky with Diamonds' and a stage costume worn by Iggy Pop.

As one of Ohio's most striking (and instantly recognisable) pieces of architecture, the 150,000-square-foot building has a glass-enclosed, double pyramid adjacent to a 162-foot tower, both of which soar above the shores of Lake Erie. Be sure to wear comfy shoes, bring plenty of cash for the car park (it is almost as expensive as admission to the RARHOF itself) and allow a full two days to visit at least (more if you are forensic about the studying of each exhibit). As well as the exhibits, a toe-tapping film details all the honourees inducted since the Hall of Fame opened. It is so overwhelming that it is almost too much to take in.

Dozens of interactive multi-media kiosks provide video and sound contributions by various artists across the rock music spectrum. Arrive early if you can – the RARHOF opens at 10am – as you could realistically still be on the ground floor at the end of the first day's visit.

On 7 June 1993, the Hall of Fame threw a party to celebrate breaking ground on the building site and, of course, it was the coolest construction 'topping out' ceremony in history. A host of stars including The Who's Pete Townshend, Chuck Berry, Billy Joel, Sam Phillips and Ruth Brown (to name a few) put on their hard hats. A year later, Jerry Lee Lewis performed a rocking set as the last steel beam was placed in position. Then in 1995, Chuck Berry opened a benefit show that featured James Brown, Bob Dylan, Aretha Franklin, Johnny Cash and Booker T. and the M.G.s. At the ribbon-cutting ceremony, special guests were Little Richard and Yoko Ono.

Outside, a 65,000-square-foot outdoor plaza is a venue for live performances – the plan is to stage more of these in the future, in order to cement the RARHOF as a destination attraction. Today 90 per cent of visitors to the musical Mecca live outside of Cleveland. Many schedule a trip to coincide with a big-name concert at the city's main arena or small bands at the House of Blues.

Contacts:
Rock and Roll Hall of Fame
rockhall.com

This Is Cleveland
thisiscleveland.com

NEW YORK CITY, USA

Wherever they are around the globe, music-lovers are sure to remember the moment when they heard the news of John Lennon's tragic death. It was the night of 8 December 1980 and Lennon was in the city he had made his second home – New York. Though born and bred in Liverpool, England, Lennon had chosen New York for the freedom and relative anonymity it offered him, away from the prying eyes of the British tabloid press and the demands of superstardom. In the buzz of the Big Apple, Lennon felt less inhibited by his fame and he would enjoy walking around Greenwich Village with its artists, vegan cafés, political activists and book stores. With Yoko Ono by his side, Lennon had initially based himself in a suite at the St. Regis Hotel at East 55th Street. Located in the heart of Manhattan, the elegant St. Regis, with its plush guest rooms and bespoke-furnished suites, offered the former Beatle a refuge from screaming girls and paparazzi. Later the couple moved to an apartment on Bank Street, but moved out when it was burgled. They secured an apartment at The Dakota, a fine building opposite Central Park and it was here, at 1 West 72nd Street, that star-snapper Annie Leibovitz took the iconic photograph for the 1981 cover of *Rolling Stone*. It was one of the few times Lennon had allowed a photo shoot in his home and within a few short hours he was dead. He was murdered outside The Dakota by a delusional, born-again Christian from Texas who idolised him. Mark Chapman fired at Lennon five times, and remained at the crime scene by Lennon's body, where he began reading *The Catcher in the Rye*, by J. D. Salinger, awaiting arrest. The police took Chapman away without incident and Lennon was pronounced dead at St Luke's Roosevelt Hospital at 23:07 that night.

Some of John Lennon's favourite places to hang out in NYC include a recording studio on West 48th Street – The Hit Factory. On the sixth floor is where he and Ono collaborated on album, *Double Fantasy*. Although the studio has changed hands, Yoko Ono continues to work there and the building contains some Beatles memorabilia. A short walk away, on 8th Avenue, is the place where Lennon loved to eat lunch – the hamburgers at Smith's Bar are legendary amongst musicians with late-night cravings and rumbling stomachs.

Just a stroll away from The Dakota, in the leafy environs of Central Park, between 71st and 74th Streets, you'll find Strawberry Fields, a tranquil spot where Lennon often liked to spend time. After his death, the location became a designated Quiet Zone for peaceful contemplation and meditation in honour of John Lennon and his pursuit of peace. The area was re-landscaped by the Central Park Conservancy with the help of landscape architect Bruce Kelley and a generous $1 million donation from Yoko Ono. It was officially dedicated to his memory on 9 October 1985 – the 45th anniversary of his birth. A circular black-and-white tiled mosaic, embedded into the pathway and surrounded by towering elms, bears the word 'Imagine' in reference to one of his most poignant songs of peace. Benches set around the mosaic provide a place to stop and ponder, which millions of tourists do each year: taking time away from the hubbub to relish the hush of the memorial and the poems, talismans and flowers left here.

Strawberry Fields is named after the title of the Beatles' song 'Strawberry Fields Forever,' a track recorded in 1966 and inspired by the childhood memories of John Lennon, who used to play in the garden of a Salvation Army children's home called Strawberry Field. His aunt, who raised him, disapproved of Lennon playing there without permission, though Lennon would insist it was 'nothing to get hung up about' – a famous lyric in the song.

Immortalized by the iconic black and white design, created by a team of artists from the Italian city of Naples, the mosaic at the Strawberry Fields memorial evokes a vision and hope for a world without strife, war and conflict. Nearby, a bronze plaque lists the more than 120 countries that planted flowers and donated money for the maintenance of the area as an endorsement of the land as a Garden of Peace. As a living memorial, sprouting leafy shrubs, flowers, boulders and rocks characterise this corner of Central Park, which is a popular pilgrimage point on Lennon's birthday (9 October) and the anniversary of his death (8 December). On these dates each year, a spontaneous singing of Lennon songs often lasts well into the night. Candles and lanterns are lit, and prayers said, by music fans from all over the world.

One of New York's most famous addresses in Pennsylvania Plaza, Madison Square Garden, also boasts the distinction of being the venue where Lennon made his last major live appearance. Joining Elton John on stage on 28 November 1974, a month after Lennon's album release of *Walls and Bridges* – the LP that produced the only No. 1 single in his solo career, 'Whatever Gets You Thru the Night', Lennon sang the single as a duet with Elton John on backing vocals and piano, as well as 'Lucy in the Sky with Diamonds', and 'I Saw Her Standing There'.

Other sites of note with a Lennon connection in New York include galleries in Greenwich Village and the Pink Tea Cup, an eatery well away from the fame machine. Lennon would enjoy lively debates about the Vietnam War with friends who lived on Prince Street, next door to the

Photo: Jorge Láscar

Vesuvio Bakery. He would enjoy good strong coffee and flick through a newspaper in Café La Fortuna, just around the corner from The Dakota – now a hardware store. Lennon also took son Sean for swimming lessons on 92nd Street where he felt like just another face in the crowd – not a former Beatle. He enjoyed walking around New York with his wife and young son, picnicking in Central Park and enjoying the spiritual embodiment of this wholly unique city. He loved its gritty urban side, its green spaces and its intellectual community and admired the character of New York City intensely. Yoko Ono refused to turn her back on the city despite the horror of Lennon's death: she remained in The Dakota and dedicated herself to spearheading the creation of Strawberry Fields in her husband's honour. Of course Lennon's music is the greatest memorial of all, but Strawberry Fields is a remarkable legacy: a place of songs, vigils and spontaneous tributes that was a natural gathering place for fearful New Yorkers in the wake of the terror attacks of 9/11. It is always populated with people: thinking, smiling and appreciating the seasons – proof that a memorial can transcend all expectations and become so much more than a monument to a single person, but a symbol of hope.

Contacts:
Rock Junket Tour of New York
rockjunket.com

New York Music Tours
city-discovery.com

Rock, R&B and Hip Hop Tours of NYC
hushtours.com

MONTREAL, CANADA

The late great Leonard Cohen had a deep and complex relationship with his home town, Canada's cultural capital Montreal. When he came into the world in 1934, Montreal was fizzing with underlying tension as a growing number of Jewish factory owners, lawyers and doctors arrived in the city. His family were prosperous with their roots in suit-making and tailoring and Cohen grew up around Murray Hill as it was then (today it is known as Westmount), on Belmont Avenue in the plushest part of affluent Mount Royal. From here, a young Cohen would stroll down Côte St. Antoine to Shaar Hashomayim, the synagogue where his forefathers had worshipped for some 150 years. Cohen also had his bar mitzvah here, and it was where he said *Kaddish* (a mourning prayer) for his dead father when he was only nine.

In his songs, he visited this familiar part of Montreal in his lyrics with a degree of frequency and drew on the power of a Jewish congregational choir and the prayers he shared with his uncles. Yet, like many of us, in the city of his birth and the cradle of his longings, he could feel both at home – cosy and warm – or as welcome as an unwanted intruder. For more than eight decades, Montreal for Cohen was both a place to escape and a refuge.

Growing up on Belmont Avenue was fun for Cohen, who would play on Murray Hill, running down its grassy slopes on summer days and skiing there in winter. Bushes, shrubs and trees offered plenty of hiding places and den space. From his bedroom window, Cohen could also see the ice rink where he would skate with friends. Though his neighbours in their large houses were families with money, at school

Photo: Exile on Ontario St

Cohen mixed with Anglophone Christians and Jews from all walks of life. Whilst studying English at the city's McGill University he published poems in a student paper called *The Forge*, and many were later included in his first collection, *Let Us Compare Mythologies*. Cohen formed a country-folk music trio at McGill called the Buckskin Boys and said at the time that he felt the need to bring poetry 'back to the jukebox, which is really where you have to have it, or at least where I like to have it'. Once he had graduated, he tried his hand at working in the family's clothing business – a job that didn't last long. In 1956, he moved to New York to continue his studies at Columbia University, but dropped out to devote himself to a career in poetry.

Today, in Montreal there is still a strong sense of the city's history. Cohen often remarked on this aspect of his hometown's character, poignantly noting: 'In Montreal there is no present tense, there is only the past claiming victories.' Montreal still has a huge number of bars and clubs, some bright and airy and others neon-lit and seedy. Cohen's first public performance was in one of the down-at-heel places, the Birdland jazz club above Dunn's Delicatessen. It was 1958 and with an improvised piano accompaniment, Cohen recited a poem in a form of delivery made fashionable by Beat poets. Today, most of Cohen's downtown haunts are gone, including Le Bistro (the Parisian-style bar where he met Suzanne Verdal, the nominal inspiration for his song 'Suzanne'). However, you can stroll along Stanley Street to see where he rented an apartment and used it as an informal art gallery. Until, that is, it caught fire and turned to ash. In several of his works, Cohen refers to the Virgin Mary that stands atop Notre-Dame-de-Bon-Secours Chapel – a church that is also known as the Sailor's Church today and can be seen in

Montreal's Old Port. Dunn's Birdland, and virtually all of the old club district, including Cohen's favourite hang-out at De Maisonneuve and Metcalfe, has been memorialised in a McCord Museum (musee-mccord.qc.ca) display after the original building was demolished. The synagogue is still there, of course, as are various members of Cohen's family: you'll find his uncle's name (Horace) in a couple of the prayer books in the Cohen family pew. His family's faith, and his fascination of spiritual themes, is undoubtedly what lies behind his exploration of religious paradoxes and moral dilemmas, such as spirit and flesh; elevation and shame; the holy and the carnal. It has often been said that there is always a lot of wisdom in a three-minute Leonard Cohen song, even if much of it is ambiguous. Cohen certainly had the skill to turn both personal, dark experiences and banal ordinary incidents into beautifully crafted poetic tales.

Successive books of verse, and especially his two experimental novels (*The Favourite Game*, published in 1963; and *Beautiful Losers*, which followed in 1966) made Cohen a literary star in Canada. He travelled to Greece, Great Britain and Cuba (his visited famously coincided with the Bay of Pigs invasion). His debut album, *Songs of Leonard Cohen*, came out in 1967 with follow-up *Songs from a Room* charting well in England and the US in 1969. Critics would pore over his lyrics, rolling them around their mouths and marvelling at their precision. Cohen was drawing on themes of love and loss and desire but in a whole new way – and it pleased them, mainly. Chords resounding, words powerful but sparing, simple and pure. His reputation dipped during the disco years of the '70s – Cohen's 1984 album *Various Positions* was refused by an executive at Columbia Records, his long-time label. 'Leonard, we know you're great, but we don't know if you're any good', they told him. The disc contained 'Hallelujah' which became one of Cohen's best-known and most-performed songs. Taking him two years to write, 'Hallelujah' has appeared in the movie *Shrek* and has been used by TV shows that include *The West Wing*, *ER*, *Scrubs*, *Holby City*, and *The OC*. When it was recorded by *X Factor* winner Alexandra Burke, it became the fastest selling download single in history. Cohen earned around £1 million in royalties from sales of Burke's version. Rufus Wainwright sang it in the Leonard Cohen tribute film, *I'm Your Man*, and it has also been covered by hundreds of other artists including Bob Dylan, Bono, k.d. lang, Justin Timberlake, Bon Jovi and Jeff Buckley. 'Hallelujah' originally had 80 verses, fifteen of which were used. Cohen has recorded two versions – the second one appeared on a live album in 1988 and both had very different endings; one upbeat, one dark. The song is broadcast at 2am every Saturday night by the Israeli defence force's radio channel. Cohen has said of the song's meaning: 'It explains that many kinds of hallelujahs do exist, and all the perfect and broken hallelujahs have equal value.'

Today, 'Hallelujah' is exalted for its honeycomb of gorgeous lyrics that can be traced back to Cohen's upbringing living amongst broadly different religious-linguistic cultures that rubbed each other the right way. That a song of such clarity was written by a gruff, brilliant, intellectual fascinated by a messiah's divinity, disciples and sacrilegious saving grace seemed improbable, somehow. 'And it's not a cry that you hear at night. It's not somebody who's seen the light. It's a cold and it's a broken Hallelujah.'

Though he would eventually spend more time in the US once his career took off, Cohen's lyrics talked mainly of Montreal and the city he knew so well. He settled down with partner Suzanne Elrod in a rented flat in St Laurent, overlooking Parc du Portugal and had two children – son Adam (in 1972) and daughter Lorca (in 1974). The couple eventually bought a house nearby, which Cohen still owned when he died in 2016. The simple grey-brick property had none of the obvious superstar trappings: no Ferrari in the drive, no gilded doorway, sober grey paintwork and no sign of bullet-proof shutters. During the 1990s, Cohen spent five years in a Zen Buddhist retreat in California. He said later that the experience helped dispel the depression that had afflicted him all his life.

In 2016, the world bade Leonard Cohen goodbye at the age of 82. The outpouring of sorrow that followed hailed him as one of the world's revered and prolific visionaries. It also acknowledged Cohen's deep suspicion of fame, the media and the paradox of celebrity. Detractors criticised his sluggish tone, his tortured soul and his oracle-like cosmic narrative. Yet whether he liked it or not, and despite what the critics claimed, Cohen was a legend and an icon. He would often dismiss his talent – in 1993, he joked, 'Only in Canada could somebody with a voice like mine win vocalist of the year.'

To walk in Cohen's footsteps in Montreal one just needs to explore the city and its many literary festivals, arts clubs, libraries and cultural attractions. Montreal is an easy place to spend time in, with more restaurants per capita than any other city in North America. Winters are frosty, summers hot and humid and the city has a bird-rich botanical garden filled with colourful blooms right in its centre. Just like the French, Montrealers are known for their style, and their city offers retail destinations to match. Festivals take place year-round, not just in the summer months – and there are more than 100 in total. There are museums and galleries for every fan of art, culture, history or science as well as outdoor theatres, opera and ballet (there are more than 250 theatre and dance companies in Montreal). Marvel at the architectural sweep of the city, which takes in a wealth of handsome styles and heritages – the dual French-English mix adds dynamism to its beauty as does its unique mash-up of European and North American culture. By the Parc du Portugal, near Marie-Anne Street, Cohen's duplex home remains enshrined by gifts, notes, wreaths, garlands and tributes. He famously once said that he became a musician when he realised musical poetry made more money than the spoken word. After setting his poems to music, Cohen's writing reached considerably more people – and some of his very finest songs were written at the kitchen table in this unassuming duplex. According to his wishes, Cohen was laid to rest at the Shaar Hashomayim synagogue in a traditional Jewish rite beside three generations of his family, hours before his death was made public; unsettled earth covered by fallen brown leaves in front of an unmarked gravestone the only evidence of his burial. 'Hineni, hineni, My Lord' and other lyrics to the song 'You want it Darker' from Cohen's final album were read at the graveside.

Contacts:
Montreal Tours
montrealtours.net

Leonard Cohen
leonardcohen.com

Visit Canada
visitcanada.com

KINGSTON AND SAINT ANN, JAMAICA

In one way or another, the Caribbean island of Jamaica pays homage to its homespun hero Bob Marley every single day. Marley's image and music is everywhere, despite it being well over three decades since the reggae legend's death in 1981, aged 36. Yet on 6 February every year the island's celebrations take on added significance as concerts, recitals and festivals honour his birth. When Robert Nesta Marley came into the world in 1945 at 2.45am in Jamaica's Saint Ann Parish nobody imagined he would grow up to become the globally recognised, Grammy-winning godfather of reggae. Yet Marley helped to propel reggae to worldwide popularity with his smoky tenor voice and loping beat. In 1964, he formed The Wailers with Peter Tosh and Bunny Livingston, recording 'Stir It Up' (1978), 'No Woman No Cry' (1975) and 'Uprising' (1980). He mixed his rhythmic pulses with a strong political message, reinforcing non-violence. He also endorsed the Rastafarian religion to become reggae's seminal figure and foremost practitioner and emissary.

Jamaica is the Caribbean's third-largest island and also one of the most colourful, with powdery white sand beaches and vibrant tropical blooms on a backdrop of hazy-blue mountain peaks. In vibrant Kingston, Tuff Gong and the Bob Marley Museum commemorate Jamaica's musical heritage, but it was once a studio, established by Marley in 1965. Another popular site is Marley's mausoleum at Nine Mile Museum in the parish of Saint Ann, several hours outside of Kingston. Each year on Marley's birthday, pilgrims from around the world gather at both sites to honour the reggae

Photo: Enrospr

legend. Some simply pop open a Red Stripe, Jamaica's favourite beer, as a tribute to the maestro. Others crank up Marley's debut release track, 'Judge Not', to acknowledge his prosperous and uplifting career. Or some simply find a reggae-drenched local bar in which to celebrate the root of Marley's music – the island and the red, green and gold of Rastafarian culture itself.

On special anniversaries Jamaica positively pulsates with the fervour of One Love: One Bob Marley. In 2015, the island celebrated what would have been Marley's 70th birthday, festooning streets across Jamaica with Rastafarian flags and bunting. Nine Mile, the rural mountain settlement where Bob Marley was born, welcomed an influx of reggae-pilgrims keen to honour the dreadlocked musical icon. For months the loping, rhythmic boom-boom beat-bouncing bass of Marley's unmistakable musical genre played homage to Bob Nesta Marley and his legions of fans. Tributes continued dawn until dusk on Jamaica's 'Remember Bob Marley Day' on 6 February, with poems that tugged on the heartstrings of scores of reggae fans from across the globe. Today, roses are placed around the many statues that honour his talent on practically any day of the year.

Marley's charismatic, loose-limbed stage presence is captured beautifully in bronze monuments across Jamaica – though the most-visited tends to be the one at the Bob Marley Museum, housed in singer's former home in Kingston town. Ethiopian Orthodox clerics, Rastafarian brethren, old friends, family members and tourists alike gather around the property on dates throughout the year, from the date of Marley's first record release to his spiritual awakening. Candle-lit reggae jam sessions take place to coincide with posthumously released live recordings or bizarre occasions such as the launch of Ben & Jerry's special-edition Bob Marley ice-cream flavour 'Satisfy My Bowl': a mouth-watering concoction of banana ice cream beats, a mash-up of caramel and cookie swirls, and a chorus of chocolatey peace signs dedicated to a man whose music practiced togetherness and harmony.

A Bob Marley reggae musical, created by the Jamaica Musical Theatre Company (JMTC) and Tuff Gong International, is still performing to sell-out crowds. Called 'Nesta's Rock', it tells the story of the childhood of a boy from the slums who embarks on a journey to Nine Mile and on to musical superstardom. Moving adaptations of some of Marley's biggest hits play a starring role in the production, including spellbinding versions of 'Redemption Song', 'Three Little Birds' and 'Could You Be Loved'. The cast is comprised entirely of native Jamaicans between the ages of nine and 21 and has the full backing of Marley's daughter Cedella, who he charged with protecting his legacy. Not every reggae musician has been able to change cultural landscapes like Marley did – and still does – and the messages of pride, love, passion, hope, peace and political strength fundamental to his best-loved anthems continue to reach out and touch the world – not just the disenfranchised youth of the Trench Town ghetto.

Looking for a comfortable way to pay tribute to Bob Marley? Jamaica's upscale hotel properties owned by Chris Blackwell of Island Records fame (who signed Marley in the early seventies and found his songs an international audience) offer an upscale option for visiting reggae pilgrims. After he was buried on the island with full state honours in 1981, 'One Love' – Marley's soulful pacifist reggae lament – became the theme song of the Jamaican Tourist Board. Marley was buried with a soccer ball, his Gibson Les Paul guitar, and a bud of marijuana. In one day alone, more than

40,000 people filed past his coffin as an entire island – and the wider world – mourned their loss.

Today, holiday-makers – a mix of recording artists, producers and spirited tourists alike – are serenaded by the lyrics of this musical milestone when they explore the Bob Marley Museum, Tuff Gong studio and Marley's final resting place in the mausoleum in Nine Mile in the parish of Saint Ann. You'll see items that reflect his daily life, such as his hammock, brightly-painted frescoes, his herb garden and the much-loved battered Land Rover he drove around the island. Other memorabilia includes including original newspaper clippings saved by the man himself. Ya mon.

Contacts:
Bob Marley Museum
bobmarleymuseum.com

Bob Marley
bobmarley.com

Jamaica Tourist Board
visitjamaica.com

RODNEY BAY, ST LUCIA

Though there is a daily concentration of Amy Winehouse fans gathered around her former home in Camden, North London, many lovers of her exceptional musical unique talent prefer to visit a place that represents happier times for the 'Back To Black' singing star. It's all too easy, they suggest, to wallow in the gloominess of Winehouse's highly publicised drug and alcohol addictions. In the darkest days of her self-destruction, Winehouse was often photographed by the tabloids in and around the London streets where she lived: bruised, bloody and incoherent after another shambolic night on the town. Frequently spotted in the Hawley Arms pub, her favourite local Camden haunt, Winehouse eventually took advice and sought sanctuary in the palm-fringed sands of St Lucia. It was here that the smoky-voiced singer, who won five Grammy Awards and who Elton John hailed 'one of the greatest artists this country has ever produced', could relax and be herself and enjoy the slow-paced Caribbean vibe. A beguiling mix of strength and fragility, Winehouse had a heart of gold yet suffered from incredible self-doubt, which made her emotionally vulnerable. She felt liberated in St Lucia, over 4,000 miles away from her musical legacy in a laid-back tropical paradise far away from the pressures of fame.

St Lucia certainly is a beautiful Caribbean island in which to escape the rat race with its lush, foliage-rich scenery as inviting as its gorgeous sands. Winehouse was wowed by mountainous terrain covered in a blanket of thick rainforest and, like legions of travellers before her, totally seduced by the green and precipitous volcanic cones of the Petit Piton and Gros Piton, rising out from the sparkling blue depths. It is the sort of island that travellers to the Caribbean fantasise about – a small, lush, tropical gem that is still relatively undeveloped. As one of the Windward Islands of the Lesser Antilles, St Lucia is located midway down the Eastern Caribbean chain, to the north of Barbados in between Martinique and St. Vincent. At only 27 miles long and fourteen miles wide, with a shape that is said to resemble an avocado, St Lucia boasts golden sands in the north, silvery

Photo: Vlad Podvorny

beaches in the volcanic south and secluded coves with a romantic feel.

In and around the livelier Rodney Bay Village, Amy made friends with the locals and enjoyed the island's special charm. Over the weeks, she formed a very special bond with a woman who she called her 'second mama'. Marjorie Lambert is a born-and-bred St Lucian who owns a little shack that serves authentic home-cooked Caribbean food on the beach. Funny, genuine and warm, Marjorie has a knack for putting people at ease. Amy felt immediately comfortable with this straight-talking mother figure who helped her recuperate on the island and they soon became firm friends. Today Marjorie Lambert still runs the rustic Cas-en-Bas bar next to Cotton Bay Village Resort in Rodney Bay, where Amy lived on and off for almost three years. Reached by a bumpy dirt track, this on-the-water bar is hidden from prying eyes. With a menu of Caribbean soul food, Marjorie's bar was the place Winehouse loved the most. She'd gaze out over the surf, wiggle her toes deep in the sand and lose herself in the quietude of the seascape. According to Marjorie, her daily tipples were Red Bull and Lucozade – a far cry from the 'Rickstasy' she ordered in the Hawley Arms, a potent concoction of three parts vodka, one part banana liqueur, one part Southern Comfort, and one part Baileys. However, despite signs that her prolonged stay on the island was helping to rid Amy Winehouse of her demons, she was unsteady on her feet when she took to the stage at St Lucia's annual jazz festival. Far from being relaxed, she looked pale and strained, quitting the stage early after slurring through half the set list and stumbling around the stage. As she muttered into the microphone 'I'm bored', by way of explanation, the crowds booed and jeered. Fleeing the venue, Amy headed back to seek comfort and reassurance from Marjorie and her family, and the local kids playing on the beach flocked to her when she arrived, throwing their arms around her as she wept. She was inconsolable as she knew she had let her local fans down, and the event marked the start of a serious decline in her health. Just a little over two years later Amy Winehouse was dead.

Today, not far from where she lived in Camden, UK, at the Stables Market, a life-size bronze statue memorialising Amy Winehouse is a gathering point for fans each day. Created by artist Scott Eaton, the monument stands as an ode to the talent of the singer: it is sassy, petite and includes her signature sky-high beehive. At 30 Camden Square, her former home, Camden Council have repeatedly appealed to Winehouse fans to stop stealing the road signs. Well over fourteen replacement signs have been erected since her death, costing over £290 a pop. Other London-based sights with a Winehouse connection include the Jewish Museum, where there is a permanent exhibit, and the Roundhouse, a music venue that was once a railway engine shed, where Winehouse played her last ever UK gig. A £30 million dilapidated mansion at 33 Portland Place, Marylebone in London is the video location for Winehouse's hit single 'Rehab', while Abney Park Cemetery in Stoke Newington was the setting for the video for 'Back to Black'.

Contacts:
St Lucia Tourist Board
saintluciauk.org

Amy Winehouse
amywinehouse.com

CARTAGENA, COLOMBIA

Few countries on earth boast a history as compelling as Colombia: a dramatic story with a gripping plot full of sudden twists. Colombia is South America's fourth-largest country after Brazil, Argentina and Peru and for five long decades a nationwide quest for peace has united mothers, grandfathers, children and students in hope. Finally, after a lifetime of violent conflict, Colombia has written a brand new and exciting chapter in its complex history. Today, a new era is unfolding in this most vibrant country. Tourism is up; discord is down. Optimism is running high, with hopes to match.

Colombia boasts a mix of cultures as fascinating as its diverse topography. As the only South American nation with both Pacific and Caribbean coastlines, it boasts a wealth of shoreline character, from the boggy horseshoe bays, inlets and jutting marshland peninsulas of the Pacific shoreline to the Caribbean's saline lagoons, sandy beaches and pretty outlying islands. Bordered by Brazil, Ecuador, Panama, Peru and Venezuela, Colombia has a rich stew of customs, languages, faces, traditions, music and dance. Spanning $1,141,748 \text{km}^2$ – an area double the size of France and four and a half times bigger than the UK, Colombia boasts its fair share of handsome colonial cities. Elegant facades adorned with painted shutters and ornate balconies are some of the most beautifully preserved colonial-era architecture in the Americas.

In colour-rich Cartagena, a criss-crossing of sun-bleached cobblestone paths lie shimmering in the Caribbean's sweltering heat. Set on the seductive curves of a palm-scattered shoreline, Cartagena is inextricably linked with the blue-green waters that lap its sands, coral reefs and cays. Stretching more than 1,750km, Colombia's Caribbean coastline boasts the distinction of being the first to be conquered by the Spanish. Today it not only contains Cartagena, founded in 1533, but also Colombia's oldest surviving city – Santa Marta (founded in 1525). Both lie shrouded in a sticky, steamy tropical haze with Cartagena's street-scape a more picture-perfect setting of painstakingly restored buildings in bold bubblegum hues. Facing the Caribbean Sea to the west with a sweeping bay to the south, the city is a jaw-dropping jewel-box of Spanish colonial ostentation, declared a UNESCO World Heritage Site in 1984. A flamboyant vibrancy befits Cartagena as the artistic hub of the Atlantic coastline. Today it is a city where street carnivals and parades celebrate a seemingly permanent state of festival: a character born out of a slave-trade past in which sainthood and swashbuckling buccaneers each play a part. Cartagena is best discovered by simply walking its streets. Meander to your heart's content through rectangular plazas where vendors offer juicy red papayas in giant slices. Sizzling curb-side food stalls emit the telltale aromas of Cartagena's deep-fried, meat-filled empanadas (corn-flour turnovers) while street clowns entertain *tinto*-sipping passers-by. A steady climb up to the cannon-topped ramparts allows views out to the Archipiélago Nuestra Señora del Rosario, a 100-hectare cluster of idyllic islands that sit amongst coral reefs in a conserved marine park. Once inhabited by Caribe Indians, the islands are renowned for their sea-grasses, plankton, crustaceans, fish, mangroves, seabirds and powdery beaches. Musical heritage fuses intoxicating Latino beats with booming African rhythms and dramatic European theatrics. You

Photo: Juan Esteban Villegas

can sway in a hammock to calypso rhythms, party hard to sassy salsa, leap and jump to tribal drumming and sashay to cowboy folk classics.

With so much thrilling, multi-cultural, creative inspiration running through the veins of the city, music is everywhere. Wherever you stroll in Cartagena you are sure to be serenaded, be it from the blaring radios of public transport, souped-up car stereos or the pounding sound-systems in bars, restaurants and even offices. Accordion-led *vallenato* can be heard in the shadows of El Centro while the syncopated boom-boom of Reggaetón pulsates in downtown Bocagrande. Elsewhere, in the beach bars and the budget booze joints, it is the retro salsa of the '70s and '80s with its heroes like Hector Lavoe, Celia Cruz, Willie Colón, Ruben Blades and local lad Joe Arroyo that fills the air.

Looking for the mighty soul of Cartagena's legendary music scene? Then head for the smoky watering holes near Castellano – an area the locals refer to as *Avenida de la Rumba* (meaning 'Party Avenue'). This is where Cartagena's unique style of street music dominates the airspace – welcome to the home of Champeta, Colombia's homespun rootsy dirty-dancing. This gutsy, sleazy rhythm born out of African beats began in Cartagena's backstreets, where musicians lay down tracks in an innocuous alleyway studio. It's a ramshackle set-up, with local bands and recording artists paid a few coins per song – yet the tracks are mixed within a few short hours. CDs are ready to pass around on the very same day, with city-wide distribution courtesy of Cartagena's legions of bus drivers. Copies are bootlegged by morning and lyrics learned off-pat as the latest hot Champeta hit finds its home on the lips of every working-class *champeduro*. Scandalous, salacious and provocative, Champeta was once outlawed by the city's Catholic Church elders. Disapproving parents have even sought police intervention due to the saucy nature of the lyrical content. Though it has slowly become mainstream in style, Champeta clings on to its earthy origins. To dance it is to set your butt cheeks bouncing while your knees are slightly bent and your arms are lifted up, outstretched Messiah-style. In 2005, celebrated local Champeta star John Gutiérrez Cassiani (aka 'El Johnky') was shot in gang violence. More than 8,000 dancing fans joined his funeral procession in a moving tribute that brought the streets of Cartagena to a standstill.

Contacts:
This Is Cartagena
ticartagena.com

Colombia Tourist Board
colombia.travel

LOS LLANOS, COLOMBIA AND VENEZUELA

Los Llanos (The Plains) is an expansive wilderness that forms a rolling tropical grasslands region, nourished by the Orinoco River. Stretching across into both Colombia and Venezuela, the sparsely populated savannahs are the home of the traditional *Llaneros* (plains-folk). This is South America's slow-paced 'Cowboy Country' where there are few of the gadgets used in modern farming, just vast sweeping alluvial plains grazed by livestock and devoted to cattle rearing. In both Colombia and Venezuela, Los Llanos is a byword for the heartfelt crooning of the distinctive

Photo: CIAT

song of the cattle-roping cow hand. Tearful ballads of regret and heartbreak recall tales of lost love and betrayal in traditional style, accompanied by the gentle strumming of strings. With their moustached faces, dark hair, leather chaps, boots and sombrero, the Llaneros are fiercely proud of their cowboy culture and uphold the old cattle-roping traditions and horsemanship skills that have been handed down through generations. Cattle reared on these fertile plains are sold for beef and shipped across Colombia and Venezuela or eaten locally as huge slabs, fire-grilled over a flame. You'll find steak cooked at traditional roadside eateries throughout the small towns of Los Llanos in amongst the cattle fields, haciendas and cowboy ranches. For well over three centuries, the barren lands of this region were entirely ignored by settlers who considered it to hostile to farm, such was the muggy and oppressive heat. But by the early 1840s, parcels of free or subsidised land and improved roadways helped entice farmers into the savannah's furthest reaches. These early settlers in Los Llanos were formidable horsemen with legendary equestrian skills. They fought for Spanish royalists and then joined Venezuelan and Colombian freedom-fighters during the War of Independence, crossing the Andes with Bolivar to take the Spaniards by surprise in 1819.

Today, the region is entirely different from the rest of their respective home nations in terms of its landscape, character, culture and wildlife. Together, the Venezuelan Llanos and Los Llanos Colombia forms around 17 per cent of South America's 29 million hectares of savannah ecosystem, with a musical tradition created amongst the seasonally flooded plains. Songs reflect the nomadic life of the cowboy and the bond, companionship and reliance he enjoys with his steed. Lyrics often capture the ebb and flow of the Orinoco River and the river delta region of bogs and coastal mangroves – often as a metaphor for life and love. Over 100 mammal species and 700 species of birds call Los Llanos home – yet these, and the human population, are dwarfed by 15 million heads of cattle on 1.3 million hectares of lush, green, springy grass.

Ethnically a mix of Spanish and indigenous tribes-folk, the *Llaneros* boast strong forearms, square shoulders and a strangely poetic style of speech. Their nasal, tonal dialect and dialogue is peppered with phrases unchanged from the idioms of 16th–17th century Spanish colonists, which is particularly prevalent in the *Llaneros'* tuneful romantic laments. Some of the most notable songs compare the isolation of the lonesome prairies to the loneliness of lost love. Harp-led melodies blend machismo desires with big-hearted passions and pride in surviving a tough life. *Llaneros* are dedicated to their cattle from the cradle to the grave, driving herds over many thousands of acres. During the rainy season, the cattle are driven to higher ground and the herdsmen are away from home for extended period of time. Rodeos provide a rare opportunity for the *Llaneros* to mix with other herdsman during cattle-roping, corralling, ranging and lassoing contests. It is here that the lonely, single *Llanero* hopes to find a wife after long days spent in the saddle in extreme heat and high winds. Wearing the traditional clothes of the region – always – the *Llaneros* are found in a poncho, straw hat and *cotizas* (rope-soled sandals). *Llaneros* are highly superstitious, with ancient legends and myths continuing to form an important part of modern society. Some of the most prevalent find their way into *Llanero* songs, such as the *Leyenda de Diablo* (Devil's Legend) – a devil's offer of untold riches and all the women in the world in return for a man's soul – *Bola de Fuego* (Ball of Fire)

– balls of fire of such ferocity that they can chase people into their homes – and *Jente sin Cabeza* (Headless Rider on Horseback) – a headless horseback rider wielding a machete that only appears at night-time gatherings.

On the Colombian side of Los Llanos, in the town of Villavicencio, a sign declares it as *'La Puerta al Llano'* (The Gate to the Plains) least you be unsure of its status in the region. Dubbed *'Villavo'* by its inhabitants, the city is almost entirely concerned with the business of cattle-raising, distilling, milling and saddle-making. Agricultural traders pass through region's commercial hub, arriving in one of the many gas-spewing trucks that rumble along the dusty routes from Bogota and cities in Venezuela. Alongside its modern development, Villavicencio retains the feel of a city keen to hold on to bygone traits. A lengthy tradition of oral storytelling remains a cultural backbone of societal culture with the city home to a number of seasoned narrators and storytelling events in parks, schools and plazas happening regularly. Visitors flock to the Llanero Museum with its collection of exhibits that detail the importance of music to a horse-riding herdsman. Music is, in many respects, the counter-balance to the hardships faced each day by the *Llaneros*. Music, singing and dancing is intrinsic to the existence of the Llaneros – and the way the solitary cowboy can let off steam. But it is more than this, with the musical tradition an important part of the cultural fabric of a vast part of the Colombian-Venezuelan territory. 'Love has nothing for me that my heart cannot hold … I will die on the land I love, forever a Llanero, forever a Llanero …'

Contacts:
Los Llanos Venezuela
losllanosvenezuela.com

Music of Los Llanos
losllaneros.com

Colombia Tourism
visitcolombia.net

RIO DE JANEIRO, BRAZIL

Few countries are perceived as being as bonded to music as Brazil. With its unique blend of European harmony and melody, African rhythms, Latino beats and Native American culture, the melting pot of influences from which Brazilian music is concocted is especially rich and delectable. From the ritual songs of the indigenous peoples in pre-colonial times, with their exotic blend of rattlers, shakers and panpipes, and the thumping slave rhythms from Africa, to the heart-rending ballads of the first Portuguese settlers who brought *cavaquinhos* (a ukulele-style string instrument), the *bandolim* (mandolin), bagpipes and the Portuguese guitar. Added to this fusion were imported musical styles from Europe, such as the polka, mazurka and tango, and so it is easy to see why the melodies that began to emerge from the musicians in Brazil over time were particularly exciting. Sensuous ballads from the cattle-scattered Brazilian plains also peppered the pot, together with a scattering of a brand-new intoxicating beats, called *Bossa Nova*. The result is a national repertoire that brings together harmonies, haunting refrains with unexpected blues notes and jazz rhythms, dream-like laments and fast and furious back-beats to form some of the most amazing culturally rich music in the world.

Photo: Claudney Neves

It was against this musical backdrop, in 1985, as the nation began to take its first brave steps towards democracy after a long period of dictatorship rule, that Rock in Rio was born. Never before had a country in South America staged a music event of this type – but Rio de Janeiro rose to the challenge. The neighbourhood of Jacarepaguá was transformed into a 250,000 square metre City of Rock. Across the ten-day musical feast, a staggering 1.3 million music fans were treated to a decadent series of concerts by some of the biggest names in music across the globe, with a line-up that read like a living, breathing, heart-racing Who's Who of rock history: from Queen, AC/DC, Rod Stewart, Iron Maiden and Ozzy Osbourne to James Taylor and George Benson. Top Brazilian stars like Gilberto Gil, Elba Ramalho, Rita Lee and a whole new generation of national rockers such as Os Paralamas do Sucesso, Blitz, Kid Abelha and Barão Vermelho got Rio de Janeiro partying on an entirely new level. The playlist was sublime, the mile-high sound system awesome, the lighting effects second-to-none and a highly engaged audience a part of the show. Minds and speakers were blown as the festival totally rocked the city. Rock in Rio was born – and Brazil has never looked back.

Today, some 30 years on, Rio de Janeiro eagerly awaits this much-anticipated September diary date, conserving both energy and time off work to indulge in a lifetime's worth of music in a single week. To date, a glittering roll-call of headlining stars has included Beyoncé, Muse, Justin Timberlake, Metallica, Bon Jovi, Guns 'N' Roses, INXS, Run DMC, Joe Cocker, Carlos Santana and Bruce Springsteen, transforming it from a celebration of rock to add a sprinkling of pop, blues, rap and folksy Brazilian tunes. Fans have been treated to standout sets from Florence and the Machine, B-52s, Whitesnake and Prince and have been wowed by

Neil Young, George Michael, A-ha, R.E.M, Sting, Maroon 5, Rihanna, Elton John and Motorhead. Everyone from Katy Perry and the Dead Kennedys to Stevie Wonder, Shakira and Lenny Kravitz have sent the crowds wild.

The event has grown in scale, with various reincarnations of the Brazilian festival and offshoots in Portugal, the USA (Las Vegas) and Madrid. From a line-up of 28 bands in 1985, the festival has moved from the purpose-built City of Rock to the world's largest stadium, the Maracanã. Tickets sell out in days and there are around 160 musical attractions at each festival. More than 530,000 litres of beer, 48,000 pizzas, and 280,000 hamburgers are consumed during the event, which has more than 10 million followers on social media. Each year the organisers ramp it up – there are roller coasters now and a Ferris wheel and the neon-lit marquees in a glorious rainbow of hues mirror the bright, soaring spirits of the crowds. Apart from the madcap fandom of the front row, crushed in the name of utter devotion and adulation, the audiences at Rock in Rio are a sea of joyous faces.

The festival launched a 'For a Better World' social project in 2001, working hard to garner the support of its fans in a bid to mobilise people through music. By 2016, it had planted 118,000 trees to help offset the emissions generated by the festival and adopted practices to reduce the environmental impact of Rock in Rio. At the end of the festival, once the overflowing trashcans have been cleared up, the 185 metric tons of waste is disposed of eco-style. More than 35.7 metric tons of recycled residues are sold to benefit 29 cooperatives, with 71 more tons of organic waste composted for organic fertiliser in reforestation projects. '*Por um mundo melhor!*' the crowds cheer in unison ('For a better world'), proving that the fans' adoration of Rock in Rio runs deep.

Contacts:
Rock in Rio
rockinrio.com

Brazil Tourist Board
visitbrazil.com

HAVANA, CUBA

Havana's sultry salsa scene revels in sensual seduction, in which simmering physical chemistry and overtly sexual rhythms collide in a full-on sensory assault. Meaning 'sauce' in the Spanish language, Cuban salsa is as fiery as a chilli pepper. The music is all about raw, heartfelt want and the dance presses bodies tight together in rhythmic unison. Salsa is fast, furious and brings a frenzied passion to the dance floor. With a toss of the hair and a flick of the hips, the movements add extra frisson to the intensity of the music. 'I'm drowning and I can't live without you … without your body next to me…' resonates the ultimate salsa love cry of 'Mi Todo' ('My All'): an intimate cocktail of intoxicating lyrics and irrepressible sweat-drenched beats.

Cuban music has its roots in the *cabildos,* a form of social club among African slaves brought to the island during colonial times. Over time, the percussion used in the Santería religion's rituals were added to the music, including shaken maracas and drum patterns (*toques*). Flamenco rhythms from Spain were incorporated, and musical influences from the United States and Jamaica added to the mix. Today, the Cuban music found in Havana's Latin jazz cafés, concert halls, cabarets or bodegas is some of the world's most infectious, and it's defining characteristic is a bass pulse that comes before the downbeat, giving a distinctive rhythm known as the anticipated bass. This rich, fertile mixture of African rhythms, European melody and verse and Caribbean-Creole verse forms part of the marriage between the African drum and the Spanish guitar. Salsa dancing (called *'Casino'* in Cuba) is the most popular dance style in Cuba, and the talented musicians that create the music – using instruments such as congas, timbales, bongos, bata, maracas, *guiro*, guitar, double bass and piano – are held in high regard in traditional Cuban culture. With cigars clamped between their teeth, in the atmospheric, smoky bars of Havana, each seasoned musical maestro celebrates the nation's indelible music history. For Cuba has created a cadre of fine classical musicians and a range of ensembles that vow to preserve the integrity and spirit of the sound.

Any music-lover in Havana should experience Tropicana, the Lido-type extravaganza of Cuban music that continues to host live bands nightly. Or for an authentic night with the locals, head to Casas de la Trova, reached via cobble stoned alleyways through ancient squares that are home to domino-players, handsome colonial mansions and lines of battered old Chevrolets. In fact, nearly every restaurant in Havana has local musicians in residence, either playing Cuban jazz *à la* the Buena Vista Social Club or hot-blooded salsa at La Zorra Y El Cuervo Jazz Club. Some of the tiniest bars transform into truly intimate venues after dark and it seems that there are world-class musicians in every café. People sing in the street, waiting for the bus, or waiting on tables and you'll often find a band playing in the central plaza. Musicians also play spontaneous gigs as they stop to chat with friends over rum or coffee. Cubans love to entertain, and don't

Photo: © Nevit Dilmen

necessarily need audiences in order to strike up the sassiest dance beat as the city's *salsatecos* begin to fill. Entering a salsa bar in Cuba can be like joining a theatrical production, where the dance floor is the stage and the *salseros* the actors, as 'Lust, Pleasure, Love and Jealousy' plays out. To the 1-2-3-touch, 5-6-7-touch of a pulsating, syncopated beat a moving sea of dancers revel in physical, musical and philosophical synch. Through shifting moods and tempos, couples sustain an intense level of inter-body communication as tendrils of salsa passion ignite – and the crowds go wild.

Havana is famous for its numerous places to take a dirt-cheap salsa lesson (less than $10), pulsating venues, festivals and a year-round calendar of upcoming events. Even the shabbiest basement bar has a pocket-sized dance-floor that can sizzle with a shock of sensual energy. That music can provoke such a blaze of highly coordinated, fast-paced spins and body-to-body sashays in a salsa throng is utterly mesmerising. In the midst of the city's Cuban hustle, these skilful practitioners of fast, flash footwork dance to Cuba's most evocative grooves. It is exciting, sexy and flamboyant with lots of dips, spins and drops, and can dazzle the spectator. It may start slow, break into a core salsa rhythm, then settle into a beautiful call-and-response vocal pattern – sometime interwoven with reggae, rap and hip-hop. As the music builds and intensifies, the dancers pull into a close embrace and launch into rhythmic middle-body shudders and amazing buttock trembles. Once the triple-twirls, gyrating and figures-of-eight fade into a dreamy, slow-tempo salsa *romántica*, you'll know daybreak has arrived.

Contacts:
Go Cuba
gocuba.com

Travel To Cuba
cubatravel.tur.cu

Cuban Tourist Board (Spanish language)
cubatravel.tur.cu

BUENOS AIRES, ARGENTINA

Tango music is a soul-stirring force that encourages powerful, character-driven story-telling in those that dance to it. Though it is as old as jazz, and the variety of the music as wide, there is only one true home of tango – Argentina's capital Buenos Aires. Tango and the city are synonymous terms, with tango an integral part of the Buenos Aires culture. With its sultry 2/4 or 4/4 time, and its evocative legend-steeped history, tango has fascinated music-lovers around the world since the early 1900s. For centuries music and dance has been a way to woo a partner, with few pursuits more intimate than dancing in the arms of another – and tango fizzes with sexual tension like a static overload. Feeling the music and sharing its rhythmic pulse, as bodies intertwine and role-play, can help create an intense affinity with the music. Tango is all about the thrill of human chemistry, and in the dimly lit dance-halls of Buenos Aires thousands of couples enjoy the moodiness, spark and sensuality of the melodic sounds of *orquesta típica* with violins, piano, double bass and guitar coupled with the arresting, haunting strains of the *bandoneón* (Argentine concertina).

As a UNESCO Creative City and the home of the art of sensual dance-floor seduction, Buenos Aires has a fine collection of basement bars, piano lounges and dance-halls that ooze with tantalising tango. The dance combines simmering physical chemistry with yes/no staccato rhythms and has its origins in the port-side bordellos of the city's seedy backstreets. Desire is laced with a trace of madness, nuanced by a spirited interchange between the paramours. The musicality of the tango plays this out perfectly, driving the pace of a private drama that sends couples circling round each other, lost in pulses and waves of want. Slow and slithery movements are punctuated with sharp, staccato jerks, foot flicks and head snaps in a hypnotic counter-clockwise flow. Close caresses are followed by petulant dismisses and flirtatious standoffs. Then, as the tempo and the desire intensifies, the dancers perform high-kicks, toe taps and cat-like postures, as they hold each other leg-in-leg. The music is pure melodrama: every beat and refrain ignites a fiery encounter. As couples circumnavigate the dance-floor, hand-in-hand and slowly but surely, the tango rhythm uses heightened pauses to accent a jut of the chin, a flick of the hair and the lowering of lashes. Then, as the musicians fall silent, the final beat marks a heartfelt, breathless rejection or steamy embrace.

Visually, tango is a jaw-dropping spectacle with its showcase of gorgeous figure-hugging dresses, dagger-like stilettos and slick Capone-style suits. Yet in Argentina, it is the musicians that are the superstars of the dance-floors – the power behind the passion and the lovers' lament. In every bar and highly-acclaimed tango school, the music is listened to attentively, not merely heard. There is great beauty in tango music and the interpretations it evokes have changed over time. Originating in society's underbelly during the 1880s with associations of ill repute, the tango was once considered obscene, but is now a byword for glitz and glamour.

The evolution of tango culture came when affluent families in Buenos Aires began to send their sons to Europe to study, or to do the Grand Tour. Some of these young men, having spent many happy hours in the brothels and clubs of their home town, brought the tango to polite society in Paris. The French fell in love with the music and the dance, and soon the whole of Europe had been touched by tango-mania. Historians consider 1913 the Golden Age of tango – and certainly, the impact back in Buenos Aires was profound. Once rejected by the elite as immoral, the tango was accepted into the social circles of Argentina's most wealthy. Tango musicians had been largely self-taught until then, but the most educated and classically trained musicians then began playing the tango, as orchestras began to earn a reputation for their showman skills. The dance matured too, becoming a subtle, heady blend of sex and chess. Composers, arrangers, lyricists and singers all hit new heights as concert audiences increased and the music became fashionable in film and on records.

Today, tango is one of the great world music genres, and Buenos Aires is a city that remains drenched in European cultural influences. Often referred to as the 'Paris of the South', with its street cafés, handsome buildings and wine bars, the city is home to events staged by long-running tango percussion group La Bomba de Tiempo, who appear at Konex every Monday. For tango concerts and lessons head to La Viruta or Sr. Duncan and for tango showcases check out storied Café de los Angelitos. The city remains awash with tango shows, *milongas* (events for social dancing), tango schools, tango-themed cafés and hotels, tango tours and even dial-a-tango-partner agencies, with plenty of opportunities to hear incredible tango music performed by the city's top musical pros. Arrive in the Argentine capital

Photo: Icaroamendes

in August and the World Tango Festival and World Cup could well be in full flow across a wide range of venues city-wide. As well as hotly-contested competitions, there are shows, classes, *milongas* and live tango orchestras that attract dancers and musicians from all over the world. In May each year, Buenos Aires plays host to the City Tango Championships and every *tanguerías* (venues hosting tango shows) ups its game to draw maximum crowds. Some of the smaller casual bars are big on atmosphere, such as the Cafe Tortoni, El Faro and El Querandi. Visitors to Buenos Aires can also listen to tango music all day by turning in to FM 92.7, a local station devoted to the music of the city's most emblematic tango orchestras. What is considered to be the first great tango was written around 1905 by Angel Villoldo, a solo singer with a guitar – and 'El Choclo' remains a distinctive instantly recognisable tango that is much admired.

Contacts:
Music Tours Argentina
musictoursargentina.com

Argentine Tango Tours
argentinatango.com

Walking Tours of Buenos Aires
buenostours.com

JALISCO, MEXICO

It is often claimed that the very spirit of Mexico's rich culture runs hot in the veins of her mariachis. Like the bullfighter, the mariachi is a symbol of nationalism and culture in Mexico. There is great national pride in these beloved musical icons that serenade the boulevards, public squares and sidewalks of a nation with a brand and style of music that is both storied and unique. Resounding trumpets, soaring violins and impassioned vocals typify mariachi music. Originally played by ensembles in the plaza of each community, mariachi has formed the musical heart of many towns and villages throughout Mexico. Musicians would stand on makeshift wooden platforms that served as a stage, elevating the band above the audience in the tiny settlements not far from Guadalajara in the state of Jalisco in Mexico's west-central region. Flanked by the Pacific Ocean on the western side, Jalisco is rich in maritime, folkloric and cultural traditions. Wooden instruments have long been played here, crafted from the *pilla* or the *cirimo* tree. Two violins, two trumpets, one Spanish guitar, one *vihuela* (a high-pitched, five-string guitar) and one *guitarrón* (a small-scaled acoustic bass) forms the basic mariachi band – though an ensemble of twenty isn't uncommon.

Spanish conquistadors invaded the region in about 1526 and Jalisco retains plenty of colonial heritage. However, in the hearts of Mexicans country-wide, Jalisco is primarily renowned as the region where tequila is made from the juice of the agave cactus in distilleries set in amongst the cattle fields, textile mills and forests. Tequila and music go hand-in-hand and Jalisco's biggest consumption of the liquor occurs

Photo: Jose Luis Martinez Alvarez

during its famous ten-day mariachi festival in September each year. This is mariachi on an epic scale: with mammoth stages, huge parties, contests and pageants. Concert halls, marquee tents and smaller venues stage a wide variety of different shows with the lavish parade through the middle of town the family-oriented highlight. Hundreds of different mariachis perform in sharp suits with shiny buttons from a moving cavalcade of vehicular floats. It is loud, with music pumped through mega-watt speakers as throngs of cheering spectators go wild.

The mariachi sound, known as *son*, is a distinctive musical blend of Spanish, native and African traditions exemplified by the beloved mariachi piece 'La Negra'. It is played in the wandering style of the itinerant labourer on a Mexican *hacienda*, who strolls from town to town singing songs of revolutionary heroes and enemies. One of the first large-scale public venues played by a mariachi band for a fee was San Pedro Tlaquepaque – the summer hang-out of Guadalajara's most affluent residents. It was danced using a heel-to-toe technique originated in Spain, when boots are dug into the dance-floor in a pounding, syncopated rhythm that echoes the band. Another typical mariachi dance, the *jarabe tapatio* (hat dance) became another favourite and has since been adopted as Mexico's national dance. Mariachi has become highly stylised, using prescribed movements and classic costumes, with men wearing the smart buttoned Jalisco horsemen's jacket (*charro*) and women a hand-woven shawl over a brightly-coloured sequined skirt of petticoats.

Until the 1930s, mariachi groups were very much a Jalisco folklore tradition, unknown outside the region. However, when President Lázaro Cárdenas invited a mariachi band to play at his inauguration in Mexico City 1934, the music was thrust into the spotlight. Written music evolved which was then shared amongst different mariachi bands and recorded by Mexico's most popular singers, such as Pedro Infante, Lola Beltran and José Alfredo Jiménez. As the popularity of radio, television and the movies grew, mariachi became more deeply embedded into Mexican culture. During the Golden Age of Mexican cinema (1946–1955) the biggest-selling mariachi band Vargas de Tecalitlán appeared in over 200 movies. This reinforced the well-groomed mariachi image, with a waist-length jacket over tightly fitted wool trousers and well-polished riding boots. These outfits became more ornamented with embroidery, intricately cut leather designs and silver buttons in a variety of shapes – complemented by a large bow-tie, a wide belt and a large sombrero.

At Jalisco's Mariachi Festival these flamboyant costumes are cut from cloth of every conceivable colour, to bring a rainbow of guitar-slung musical bands to the gala. There simply is no finer place on earth in which to experience the sounds and colours of the mariachi tradition than in its birthplace. Today, the International Mariachi Festival of Guadalajara is the largest celebration of mariachi music – not just in Mexico, but on the planet. Apart from Mexican mariachis performing, there are a wide range of other events connected to the mariachi culture, such as special masses in the Catholic cathedral, hundreds of market stalls, an amazing array of Mexican speciality foods and visiting mariachis from as far away as North and South America, Cuba and Spain. Evening concerts play to full-capacity crowds at the historic Degollado Theater and are dazzling, high-spirited affairs showcasing Jalisco's award-winning philharmonic orchestra. Festival-goers can also stroll galleries of mariachi-inspired art at the Regional Museum, clothing stalls and numerous workshops and studios where hand-crafted boots, instruments and leather belts are made. There are also plenty of atmospheric, dusty bars offering tequila tastings just a few miles from the fields of blue agave plants in the fertile agricultural area that surrounds Guadalajara.

Contacts:
Visit Mexico
visitmexico.com

Music Tours in Mexico
tourbymexico.com

AFRICA

STONE TOWN, ZANZIBAR

Fans of British rock group Queen and, in particular, its flamboyant lead singer Freddie Mercury, have several pilgrimage options, with the most popular choice a former home under London's Heathrow Airport flight path. The on-stage antics of this most theatrical showman and his prowling, prancing persona won Mercury worldwide adoration: he was, quite simply, an unequalled one-off. Yet few of the fans who followed him closest knew of his privileged beginnings in Africa and his exotic heritage. For Freddie Mercury – a softly spoken man with a cut-glass archetypal British accent – was born Farrokh Bulsara to Parsi émigrés on 5 September 1946, on the island of Unguja, in the Indian

Ocean archipelago of Zanzibar: a spice-growing region renowned for its abundance of cloves, nutmeg, cinnamon and black pepper.

Zanzibar has been slow to catch on to the potential tourist draw of its world-famous Freddie or to understand the lure of his hometown to devoted Queen pilgrims. So those that arrive expecting a Graceland-style extravaganza will be sorely disappointed. Retracing Freddie's youth in and around Zanzibar's capital of Stone Town is much more about discovering his old haunts than visiting a shrine: you'll walk the streets of his family, you'll see the house in which he was born, you'll feel the sentiment of the local culture and you'll understand a little about what made Freddie so out of the ordinary, so unusual, and quirky. A pilgrimage will also shed some light on his belief system, for he was raised as a Zoroastrian, as part of an ancient fire religion founded more than 3,000 years ago.

In the absence of an over-the-top tribute it is Freddie's old family home that has become the focal point. It is an unassuming brick-built house that has fallen into partial disrepair but which has clearly been maintained to stop it from deteriorating further. The result is a compromise between neglect and monument with a semi-crumbling exterior covered in Perspex in which fans from all over the world have wedged letters, drawings, scribbled poems and cards. Some are easy to read and quickly draw you in with their adoration, compassion and love. Nobody could fail to be moved by such an outpouring of heartfelt emotion.

Wandering around Stone Town gives a glimpse into Mercury's meteoric trajectory, from the springboard of a rustic island in East Africa to becoming one of the biggest pop stars in the world. Teens in Zanzibar have been encouraged to gain inspiration from Freddie's journey –

Photo: Harvey Barrison

though that it involved surviving a dead-end job washing dishes in the kitchens at Heathrow Airport is often ignored. When he was seventeen, Freddie and his family left the amazing scenery, coastline and butterfly-scattered mangrove lagoons of Zanzibar behind, fleeing a bloody revolution for London. It was 1964, and he soon settled into Feltham, playing Jimi Hendrix records in his small back bedroom. Though he didn't just listen to the music; he forensically analysed it. Dissected it. Devoured it. Not just the chords but the production technique. After meeting Brian May through the singer of his first band, Smile, life was never the same. Farrokh Bulsara, it transpired, had a truly spectacular vocal range and Freddie Mercury was born. He vowed to be a legend, assuring May he would be amazing. And he was true to his word.

In the backstreets of Stone Town, rickety wooden market stalls are stacked with counterfeit Queen CDs and street sellers touting Zanzibar souvenirs bearing Freddie Mercury's moustached face. There's a local eatery called Mercury's Restaurant in which the walls are adorned with tributes to the music of Queen. Several local tourist guides specialise in walking tours around all of the Freddie haunts of Stone Town, including the Shangani district, where he was born, the Zanzibar Gallery shop, once home to his family, and the mystical Zoroastrian temple where Mercury worshipped with his family and the local Zanzibari community. It isn't for anyone with a passing curiosity in Queen – it really is for diehard fans of Freddie Mercury the rock icon.

Zanzibar too far for a Freddie fix? Then another option is to head to the resort town of Montreux in Switzerland, the host of a famous annual jazz festival and where Queen made musical magic from 1978 to 1991. The band adored the stunning views of Lake Geneva and the relaxed atmosphere that drew world-famous musicians long before the iconic festival got started in the 1960s. Freddie began to prefer the peacefulness he found here at Mountain Studios more than London and he started to stay for longer periods at the artistic retreat. One of Queen's great collaborations, 'Under Pressure,' was written there with David Bowie in the space of just a few hours. Since Freddie's death in 1991 from an AIDS-related lung condition, the studios have relocated elsewhere in Montreux. However, the original site is now a Queen-themed museum experience, thanks to the Mercury Phoenix Trust, in which the life, the man, the group and fifteen Queen albums, two solo albums and more than ten singles are celebrated. Artefacts include handwritten song lyrics, costumes, studio tape boxes, instruments and the microphone Mercury used to record the last vocal of his career. Queen's unmistakable frontman is also memorialised in a ten-foot-tall bronze statue on the shore of Lake Geneva. Unveiled in 1996, the monument shows Mercury in his iconic pose, with a microphone in one hand and his fist pumped into the air. Visit at sunset for an incredible photo opportunity – with the light behind it, the bronze positively glows.

Every destination associated with Freddie Mercury – be it Zanzibar, Feltham or Montreux – becomes a gathering point on 5 September each year: Freddie's birthday. Expect outlandish costumes, fake moustaches, Lycra-clad tribute acts and midnight renditions of 'Bohemian Rhapsody' in which a host of spontaneous choirs attempt to recapture the complex arrangements of Freddie's most iconic song with its layers of verses, ballad section, soaring operatic passage, multi-tracked guitar, heavy rock solo, abrupt changes in tempo and rich harmonisation that will forever bring a new slant to rock.

Contacts:
Zanzibar Tourism
zanzibartourism.net

Queen Studio Experience
queenstudioexperience.com

Freddie Mercury
freddiemercury.com

LAGOS, NIGERIA

From the distorted blare of a wall of towering speakers in Lagos, Nigeria, every single sense is assaulted as a crowd pounds and pulverises a dance-floor, causing it to bounce. Nigeria's music-fuelled megacity of more than 18 million souls likes its rhythms loud, energetic and lively. An intoxicating melange of high-tempo beats has been born out of over 600 diverse Nigerian cultures. Each dance move carries history and purpose from the irrepressible hip-thrusting sashays and rhythmic shuffles to the free-spirited joyous celebrations of harvest, family and heritage.

With a rat-tat-tat, busses crash over potholes as street vendors wail and generators rattle at a machine-gun pace – an echo of the banging rhythms of its dance scene and that of Nigeria itself. Dubbed the 'heart of African music' in recognition of its trail-blazing role in the continent's music and dance evolution, Nigeria has rhythm in its blood and a throbbing drumbeat for a pulse. Much more than pure entertainment, here music and dance remain an intrinsic way to herald new life, mourn the dead, worship, rejoice, compete, love, proclaim and protest. Style, tone and tempo may vary enormously in this culturally diverse nation, yet dance still passes stories from generation to generation – as it has done for centuries. Every chorus, every move, every lyric plays a part in ensuring that cultural influences are kept alive and relevant to communities today.

With a flick of the hair, a guttural chant and a repetitive succession of rhythmic shuffles, few music and dance scenes are as utterly intoxicating as Nigeria's kicks, foot-stomps, hip thrusts, jutting chins, pouts and propeller arms. Be it the ultra-sexy *mapouka*, *makossa*'s party vibe, the ghetto-born sway of *galala*, *suo*'s hip rumble, the oh-so-vigorous *yahoozee* or the *alanta*'s crazed waggle, each Nigerian dance features an element of role-play and narrative. Nimble, agile, graceful, admirable and elegant steps combine effortlessly with down-and-dirty bump-and-grind moves as the music takes control of head, torso and limbs. Fusing native rhythms with a unique style of polyrhythm that features two or more simultaneous beats, *Naija* dance tunes can be impish, irrepressible and impossible to resist. Keen to yield to the rhythm? Then prepare for a host of spellbinding drubbing beats to whip you up into a frenzy of jerk-and-jab movements that may well leave you swaying in an awesome, syncopated trance-state.

Like other parts of the African continent, drums form an integral part of dance in Nigeria, their roots in the ancient way that rural villagers would communicate with each another across wind-carved deserts, ragged mountains and dusty plains. Across Nigeria, similar themes may be found throughout dances unique to the specific ethnic groups and landscapes, each with its own history, language, song, background and purpose, yet with common steps, beats and accompanying instruments. Over time, music has evolved

Photo: Amogunla Femi

to include brass, vocals, percussion, drums, double bass and the slow, deliberate strum of guitars, and has fused with the ancient, exotic strains of North African folk song and kettle drums. Melodious refrains hide the influence of Portuguese colonialists and modern-day reggae, calypso and jumping Zairean beats. Heavy and ongoing migration from neighbouring countries continues to add generous dollops of new ethnicity to Nigeria's heterogeneous musical melting pot with an infiltration of imported American hip-hop in recent years.

Mixing it up with social values and political mockery, Nigerian music and dance remains – in every sense – a reflection of community life. Drumbeats traditionally show the essence of the tribe (a rapid, powerful rhythm, for example, indicates a clan's vitality and strength) and bring it together. Today the relentless pounding in Nigerian dance symbolises a gathering of community. Warrior dances, which start slowly but become increasingly wild and aggressive, demonstrate the clan's might on the battlefield. Indeed many African cultures do not have a word for music and dance – it is simply a part of everyday life. Lyrics form part of a lengthy, continent-wide oral tradition, and Nigeria's fondness for elaborate costumes, masks, props, body art and gestures are part of a historic need to 'tell the story' in shared togetherness. A dance is never performed alone – it's all about kinship, participation, unity, convergence, interaction and the surging power of response.

The era of slave labour intensified the power of dance for Africans as they held on tight to the traditions of home, and developed styles to mock their masters in secret. Since slaves were prohibited from lifting their feet, they created shuffling moves, gentle body sways and a swing of the hips – movements that typify a zillion music and dance styles today.

In Nigeria, now, as in centuries past, music and dance are introduced to a child from birth. By the time they can crawl and toddle they will already be clapping, stamping, shuffling and mimicking the moves and retorts of cheeky 'calls and responses'. Next, they add leaping and jumping to their dance repertoire. As teens and young adults they may choose to embrace the music that champions their aspirations: a flashy car, a good life and a bulging wallet. Or they may opt for the traditional tunes that encourage abundant crops, mark rites of passage and give thanks.

In 2012, the Festival of African Dances chose Lagos as its venue, drawing huge crowds with a seductive programme of performances by some of the hottest musicians and dance acts from across the continent. Spurring considerable media interest Africa-wide with its dynamic display of dances of rich diversity and magnetic appeal, Nigeria further bolstered its position as a leader in African dance with troupe shows and world-class choreography until the wee small hours. Drum beats remain king in today's hip-hop, R&B and Highlife. Indeed many of today's chart hits have their origins in rhythms that date back to pre-colonial times. 'Oyato' by Nigerian singer-songwriter Dapo Daniel Oyebanjo (popularly known as D'banj) – best known internationally for his 2012 summer hit 'Oliver Twist' – used an up-tempo dance fusion of Afro-beats to top the African charts and make the top ten in the UK charts. It is still one of Nigerian radio's most played songs – and looks set to be one of the country's classic tunes. Oh-so-hip R&B singer Omawumi Megbele also uses old-style African melodies (given a mega-modern interpretation) that keep youngsters dancing 'til dawn. So did 'Gaga Crazy' by Chuddy K – a rocking party hit with a peachy, infective beat and catchy lyrics that swirled around your head all day. Combined with *Azonto* dance moves, 'Gaga Crazy' is still guaranteed to get

Nigeria dancing – much like a musical tribal ritual. Today, a growing number of Lagos venues play host to an enticing calendar of high-energy events in which an exciting mix of traditional poetry and mythological imagery accompanies a contemporary blend of old folk, R&B and dub. And trust me, it totally rocks.

Contacts:
Visit Nigeria
visitingnigeria.com

KINSHASA, DEMOCRATIC REPUBLIC OF CONGO

For decades, Congolese music has been a powerhouse of the African music scene, from rumba to ballads to *ndombolo*, and Congolese artists are legends that draw crowds to the biggest concert halls, not just in Africa, but all over the world. Music is omnipresent in the Congo: a life force that accompanies every love, lust, tearful regret, birth, death and joyous celebration. To dance to Congolese beats is to feel the nation's heartbeat after years of a violent war. Not that the country's music industry is untouched by its troubles – far from it. Between 3.1 and 4.7 million lives were lost during the late 1990s, leaving almost no family untouched. The country is devastated, ruined and divided, businesses corrupt and the state little more than a figment. Music, however, seems to be keeping the nation alive. Almost everyone can dance or sing so as the drums pound, people sway and all sense of hopelessness eases. Spirits powered by an ecstasy-given crescendo rise as the tempo soars.

Though the style of Congolese music varies across the country, once theme is common: sex. Lyrics sometimes tantalise and tease, dancing around the topic, but more often than not, songs get straight to the point. Few nationalities are as inventive as the Congolese when it comes to finding new ways to describe the carnal deed. The risqué *ndombolo* dance, itself highly sexually suggestive, has been threatened with a ban at least a dozen times – Cameroon has already outlawed the 'indecent' dance on the basis that its overtly sexual nature was corrupting young morals. So far, *ndombolo* has been banned from Congolese state radio and television, though record sales have been rampant ever since this was enforced. New releases continue to be played non-stop in smart discos, sweat-box bars and clubs across Africa: its trademark bass, tinging guitars and soaring falsettos sending pulses racing. Across Europe, this sound has almost become *the* sound of African music, with artists like the incomparable Papa Wemba in high demand.

Few Congolese musicians can compete with Papa Wemba, such is his importance to the music scene. Though he died in April 2016, fittingly on stage where he was most at home, none of the artists of the moment have been able to take his place – yet. Papa Wemba is the first star that comes to mind when thinking about Congolese music, such is his celebrity. For many people, he *is* Congolese music.

Congolese music emerged in its modern form in the early 1940s, in two cities separated by a mile of swirling brown water. War in Europe had boosted demand for Congolese copper, cotton and rubber. Factories were mushrooming in Leopoldville, as Kinshasa was called then, the capital of the Belgian Congo (now officially the Democratic Republic of Congo), and across the Congo River in Brazzaville, the capital of the French Congo (now officially the Republic

Photo: Makangarajustin

of Congo-Brazzaville). Peasants flocked to the cities from the rainforest to meet the demand for labour, bringing with them their traditional music and drums, lutes and *likembes* (a glockenspiel-like instrument played with the thumbs). An influx of 78 rpm records played a part too, with Cuban boleros, mambos, salsas and, especially, rumbas arriving courtesy of British record label His Master's Voice. Congolese labourers worked hard, and played hard: spending their money on rum and dancing to the intoxicating rhythms on their records. The first great Congolese star was Antoine Kolosay, aka Papa Wendo, a riverboat mechanic who cut his teeth singing rumbas at weddings and funerals. He wrote songs under the shade of a banana tree and soon attracted the attention of a Greek entrepreneur who seized the chance to invest in the hunger for rumba music. He built a broom-cupboard recording studio, loaned Papa Wendo instruments, and stumped up the bail when – after penning one of Congo's loveliest songs, 'Marie-Louise', a eulogy to the sister of his guitarist, Henry Bowane – Papa Wendo was jailed for satanism when Marie-Louise died.

By the mid-1950s, there were a good half-a-dozen Greek-owned recording studios, and Papa Wendo had been joined by two bands as the royalty of Congolese music. For decades Joseph Kabasele's African Jazz and François 'Franco' Luambo's OK Jazz took Papa Wendo's sound and jazzed it up, to brilliant effect. Horns and double bass were added, the lyrics became cheekier and more upbeat and soon the Congolese were buying 600,000 records a year and dancing in any one of the city's 330 bars. Then Congo's bright hopes began to fade as political fallout sparked civil war. Gone were the glory days of the nation's musical successes as money, power, greed and politics tarnished the scene. Bands split, formed factions, split and split again, forming intense rivalries in a music scene that became anarchic and demented. New bands were outlawed, the Greek-owned record companies were forcibly taken from their owners, and vinyl became a rare commodity. Clubs became churches, bars closed and there ceased to be a Congolese recording industry. Soon, 80 per cent of Congolese were living on less than $1 per day so there was no market in which to sell old copies of Congolese music records. Stars stopped performing because nobody had the money to pay – not that any of the sound systems left were up to the job.

Today Congo-based musicians rely on a bizarre style of 'sponsorship' to make money, adding the names of affluent Congolese to their songs who are then asked to pay for the privilege – even the most clever lyricist can't resist the opportunity to make cash. The Congolese enthusiasm for music is still alive and kicking, despite this, and in out-of-the-way bars the seductive sounds of Congo's music still thrives. Jupiter Bokondji is a Congolese star who in 2012 toured the UK as part of the Africa Express tour, which featured 80 musicians on one train as it made a string of stops across the UK. Bokondji, the star of *Jupiter's Dance*, a seminal documentary about the music scene in Kinshasa, has worked with Damon Albarn of Blur fame on an Oxfam music project, drawing together traditional music from all of the hundreds of ethnic groups in the DRC. While the members of his band Okwess International opted to exile themselves safely in Europe when the war started, Bokondji stayed behind, surviving Africa's deadliest conflict. As the biggest and most populous central African country at 2,345,000 square kilometres (906,000 square miles), the Congo is almost as large as Western Europe, and Bokondji was keen to play a role in keeping its arts scene going.

Today musicians Koffi Olomide and Werrason enjoy worldwide recognition and recently paid tribute to Papa Wemba during a music-filled memorial. Wemba was also posthumously awarded one of his country's highest honours from President Joseph Kabila while his body lay in state. The Order of National Heroes Kabila-Lumumba was for 'the merits, the loyal and eminent services rendered to the Congolese nation'. In his wake, a new generation of musicians such as Werra Son and JB Mina are working hard to enrich Kinshasa's *joie de vivre*. Papa Wemba, a father of six, died aged 66 after trailblazing Congolese popular music for an entire generation and leaves behind him a string of crumbling tiny clubs riddled with bullet holes on rubbish-strewn pock-marked streets. His legacy is a mix of melodic and fast, brutal dance music that is sometimes trancelike, often harsh and formed of a blend of complex beats, simple syncopations and soulful voices. Tribal and percussive, the Congolese music scene has a stronger feeling of togetherness since Papa Wemba's passing, with a new breed of young talent writing songs under the shade of Kinsasha's giant banyan trees.

Contacts:
Congo Travel & Tour Co
congotravelandtours.com

Go Congo
gocongo.com

KWAZULU-NATAL, SOUTH AFRICA

When American musician Paul Simon brought the collective voices of Ladysmith Black Mambazo to the Western world more than 30 years ago, the uniqueness of the *a cappella* gospel harmonies on his landmark *Graceland* album epitomised the South African sound. Since then, that distinctive music from the townships with its warm vocal blend showcased so perfectly on Simon's 'Diamonds on the Soles of Her Shoes' has stood the test of time. This collaboration broke Ladysmith Black Mambazo as an international act in the mid-'80s and led to global tour dates that have kept the group busy for three decades. Along the way, they have worked with an eclectic assortment of rock, folk and pop musicians who are often outclassed by Ladysmith singing all the instrumental parts – to electrifying effect.

Ladysmith Black Mambazo was formed in 1960 in the township of Ladysmith in South Africa's KwaZulu-Natal. At the time, the aim of the group was to sing at parties, births, weddings and funerals – not take the world by storm. Today they are regarded as South Africa's cultural emissaries at home and abroad, with founder Joseph Shabalala considered a 'national treasure'. Paul Simon arranged to meet Shabalala and the other members of Ladysmith Black Mambazo after being sent a cassette of their music by a Los Angeles DJ. By the time Simon met the group in a Johannesburg studio, he was captivated by the stirring sound of bass, alto and tenor harmonies. Simon's project – the Grammy-award-winning album *Graceland* – incorporated the traditional sounds of black South Africa, a watershed record that proved the catalyst to an explosive interest in world music.

Photo: Joe Mabel

Today, *Graceland*, released in 1986, is considered to be Paul Simon's crowning achievement: his eighth studio album in a stellar career. His songwriting style and clever use of poignant lyrics work wonderfully with the African folk instruments and percussive style. Ladysmith Black Mambazo sing like a choir having the perfect Sunday morning singsong. The result is an extraordinary blend of complimentary musical styles that forms a single grand creation, offering plenty of shifts in tempo and varietals of light and shade. The subtleties of Simon's thoughtful and complex album presented indigenous music to the world in a glorious way. It is hard to imagine how the song structure and mix of African rhythmic, melodic and harmonic phrasing could be improved in any way. Since *Graceland*, the sound of Soweto and its joyous and uplifting harmonies have remained on the world's musical radar.

At the time Joseph Shabalala formed Ladysmith Black Mambazo, he was a farm-boy turned factory worker. He named the group after his hometown, Ladysmith (about three hours west of Durban and three hours east of Johannesburg). Black was a reference to the oxen, the strongest of all farm animals; and Mambazo is the Zulu word for chopping axe, a symbol of the group's ability to 'chop down' any singing rival who might challenge them. By the end of the 1960s, the polished sound of Ladysmith Black Mambazo was so tight that they were banned from all local singing competitions. So they earned their money as entertainers instead. After appearing on a radio show in 1970, the group secured record label interest.

Ladysmith Black Mambazo drew its sound from the traditional *isicathamiya* (*is-cot-a-ME-ya*) music, from the black workers in the mines of rural South Africa who would break into song on the long train journeys that ferried them far away from home. Conditions were poor, the pay even worse, but singing helped raise their spirits. When the miners returned home to their families, this music returned too. During the 1970s and early 1980s it was this unique sound that helped Ladysmith Black Mambazo gain recognition and bring them to Paul Simon's attention.

After *Graceland*, the collaboration with Paul Simon continued with him producing Ladysmith Black Mambazo's first worldwide release, *Shaka Zulu*, which won a Grammy Award in 1988 for Best Traditional Folk Recording. Since then, the group has received three more Grammy Awards – for *Raise Your Spirit Higher* (2005), *Ilembe* (2009) and *Singing For Peace Around the World* (2013). The group recorded with numerous artists from around the world, including Stevie Wonder, Dolly Parton, Josh Groban, Emmylou Harris, Melissa Etheridge and many others. They also appeared on film in Michael Jackson's *Moonwalker* video and Spike Lee's *Do It A Cappella* and provided memorable soundtrack material for Disney's *The Lion King*. They have appeared on Broadway and been part of such shows as *Family Guy*. 2016 saw Ladysmith Black Mambazo – dubbed 'South African Cultural Ambassadors to the World' by Nelson Mandela – receive a nomination for Best World Music Album of 2016 by the Recording Academy for *Walking in the Footsteps of Our Fathers* – the group's 17th Grammy Award nomination. The album is a compilation of re-recorded tracks from the choir's back catalogue, a celebration of their past, present and future.

Fans of the traditional music of South Africa can visit the birthplace of Ladysmith Black Mambazo in KwaZulu-Natal on the banks of the Klip River. A former staging post for gold prospectors and miners, Ladysmith was first settled in 1850 and took its name from the wife of Governor Sir

Harry Smith. The town marks a strategic point between Johannesburg and Durban and forms the gateway to the central and northern reaches of the Drakensberg Mountains. Ladysmith hit the world's headlines in the late 19th century when it was besieged by the Boers for 118 days during a savage period in South African history. Other than the area's historical battlefields, game reserves and striking bird-rich scenery, the town is most famous for its sweet South African music. The local museum has a large collection of photographs, records, awards and documents that chronicle Ladysmith Black Mambazo's achievements. Staff can also arrange walking tours on a choral theme and can help arrange tickets to see the group perform live in venues across South Africa.

Contacts:
Ladysmith Black Mambazo
mambazo.com

South Africa Tourist Board
southafrica.net